Talk about
the Maritimes

Norman Creighton

Edited by Hilary Sircom

NIMBUS
PUBLISHING

Nimbus Publishing Limited
PO Box 9166
Halifax, NS   B3K 5M8
(902)455-4286 www.nimbus.ca

Design: Kathy Kaulbach
Front cover photo by Bob Brooks;
back cover photo by Garth Scott
Printed and bound in Canada

Canadian Cataloguing in Publication Data
Creighton, Norman, 1909-1995
Talk about the Maritimes
Originally broadcast on CBC Radio.
ISBN 1-55109-257-3
1. Maritime Provinces — Anecdotes.   2. Creighton, Norman, 1909-1995 — Anecdotes.
I. Sircom, Hilary.   II. Title
FC2028.C74 1998   971.5   C98-950196-5
F1035.8.C74 1998

Nimbus Publishing acknowledges the financial support of the Canada Council and the Department of Canadian Heritage.

Photo/Illustration Credits:

Bear River NS Fire Department and Ladies Auxiliary: 60

Conrad Byers—Time Frame Photo, Parrsboro, NS: 81

Victor Chandler, Windsor, NS: 129, 131

Charlotte County Archives, St. Andrews, NB: 77

Paul Cochrane, Edmonton, AB: 107

Alan Creighton, Toronto, ON: 169

Jan Goodlad, Windsor, NS:
2, 4, 6 (courtesy Millicent Daniels, Windsor Forks, NS)
13 (courtesy Randall House Museum, Wolfville, NS)
14 (courtesy Willow Creek Antiques, Hantsport, NS)

16 (courtesy Vaughan's Stationery and Gifts, Windsor, NS)
25 (courtesy Tamara Folker, Hantsport, NS)
26, 29, 31 (courtesy Earl & Sheila Young, Grand Pré, NS)
45, 46, 48, 49, 50 (courtesy Nova Scotia Museum)
53 (courtesy Daniel Ficza, Hantsport, NS)
64 (courtesy Sobeys)
69, 70, 71, 79 (courtesy Charles & Margot Eaves, Kentville, NS)
82, 88, 89, 91 (courtesy Jim Preston, Hantsport, NS)
92, 96, 97, 136, 149, 151, 152, 155, 159, 160, 162, 163, 166 (courtesy Randall House Museum)
101, 105, 108, 109, 110, 114, 126 (artist unknown)
129, 131 (courtesy Victor Chandler, Windsor, NS)
137 (courtesy Debbie Bowes, Windsor, NS)
138 (courtesy Shirley Curry, Folmouth, NS)
140, 141, 144, 146 (courtesy David Parsons, Hantsport, NS)
147, 148 (courtesy Betty Preston, Hantsport, NS)
167 (courtesy Tom & Joan Jones, Hantsport, NS)
168, 174 (courtesy Helen Hendry, Windsor, NS)
175, 178, 179 (courtesy Bailey & Lauren Vaughan, Windsor, NS)

Halifax Seed Company, Halifax, NS: 30, 31
Pat Heit, Halifax, NS: 3, 8, 39

Helen Hendry, Windsor, NS:
10, 32, 34, 37, 52, 86, 90, 113, 119, 139, 164, 170

Ginette LeBlanc and Fédération Acadienne de la Nouvelle-Ecosse, Chéticamp, NS: 18, 19, 20

Robert A. LeBlanc, Nova Graphics, Dartmouth, NS:
43, 68, 180

Pat McLeod, Qualicum Beach, BC:
24, 42, 58, 99, 102, 104, 106

Gary Ness, Wolfville, NS and C. P. Archives: 176

St Clair Patterson, Hantsport, NS: 153

Pictou County NS Genealogical and Heritage Society, Pictou, NS: 62

Garey Pridham—Expressions by Garey, Windsor, NS: 56

Public Archives of Nova Scotia, Halifax, NS:
5, 67, 143 (from the Helen Creighton Collection)
172 (from the B.R. Alexander Collection)

Garth Scott, NS: vii

Hilary Sircom, Hantsport, NS:
7, 12, 15 (courtesy Perry Munroe, Black River, NS)
54, 59, 61, 116, 121, 123, 150, 154, 156, 158, 161, 171 (courtesy Daniel Ficza)

Elizabeth Sircom, Le Havre, France: 21

Garth Vaughan, Windsor, NS:134

Garth Vaughan Collection, Windsor, NS: 135, 136

Christopher West, Halifax, NS: 125

West Hants Historical Society, Windsor, NS: 112

FSC
Mixed Sources
Product group from well-managed forests, controlled sources and recycled wood or fiber
Cert no. SW-COC-000952
www.fsc.org
© 1996 Forest Stewardship Council

ACKNOWLEDGEMENTS

The compilation of this book would not have been possible without the generous support and assistance of the Creighton family, in particular Jan Creighton Goodlad, administrator of the Norman Creighton estate, whose enthusiasm and expertise in many areas has kept the project on track.

Others whose assistance is gratefully acknowledged are the Dr. Helen Creighton Foundation, Halifax; Helen Hendry, Windsor; Heather Davidson, Hantsport; Charles Armour of Dalhousie University Archives, Halifax; Monica Sutherland of Pixell Wizard, Windsor; and CBC Radio.

The search for illustrations has led down some interesting paths and thanks go to all who have contributed sketches, photographs or memorabilia. Credits for these may be found on page ii.

CONTENTS

SPRING

SUMMER

INDEX OF MARITIME PLACE NAMES

Editor's Note: Most of the talks where the location is not identified describe the area in and around Hantsport, NS.

INTRODUCTION

Norman Creighton (1909-1995) was a man of many parts. He was researcher, commentator, journalist, and most importantly, a pioneer in what was during the 1940s the new field of communication—radio journalism. He is probably best remembered as the originator of the popular CBC series, "The Gillans," which was part of the daily farm broadcasts during the forties and fifties. Later, between 1962 and 1984, he could be heard each week on programmes such as "A.M. Chronicle," "Maritime Magazine" and "Radio Noon," talking about the people, places, traditions and folklore of the Maritime Provinces.

Norman Creighton, who was Norm to his friends, charmed all who met him. In his later years, he was probably best known as a "man about town"—that is, as a man about the small town of Hantsport on the River Avon, in Hants County, Nova Scotia. Here, he was a familiar figure, striding along in all weathers, knapsack over his shoulder, to the post office and grocery store. He would pass with a cheerful wave, or stop to discuss some piece of local news, to inquire about a friend's flowering crab-apple tree, or whether the smelt were running yet. Little went on in the community that did not interest him.

The Creighton house on Avon Street, where the family settled in 1937, was a haven for Norm, his sister Laleah, their dogs and numerous orange, white, and calico cats. Brother, Alan, and sister, Marjorie, also made regular lengthy visits to the family home. Here, Norm watched the changing seasons and cultivated his garden. While allowing nature to take its course as far as the profusion of snowdrops, scillas, crocuses and early bulbs was concerned, he made an effort to keep his herbaceous borders under control and took great pride in the produce of his vegetable garden and greenhouse. Most of his Hantsport neighbours can boast of offspring from Norm's perennials, for he was generous with the things he loved. At the back of the house, a tangle of fruit trees and wild roses grew down to Willow Brook. In

Norman Creighton, as gardener.

...as cat lover

Inside the house were the many, many, books, magazines, pamphlets, brochures, newspaper cuttings, and letters that provided Norm's contact with the world beyond Hantsport, and which were also the source of his livelihood. As friends and relatives discovered after Norm's death, the Creightons were tireless correspondents, who kept everything that came to them through the mail.

As a young man living in Halifax, Norm had worked at a variety of jobs before taking up shorthand and typing, which enabled him to gain steady employment as a secretary. However, he was never very strong and a bout of TB kept him at home for three years. Encouraged to be out of doors at this time, he helped his father in a nursery garden and his interest was kindled in such country pursuits as beekeeping and the brewing of cider, vinegar and mead.

In 1941, Norm took a writing course by correspondence. He had always been interested in writing and was encouraged in this by his older brother, Alan, who was by now an established writer and published poet living in Toronto. Although he doubted that he had the talent for this new career, Norm was successful in having articles accepted by several magazines and by the Canadian Broadcasting Corporation. These were the war years, when radio was in its heyday. People clustered around their sets for the latest news from the front, for the Saturday afternoon opera from the Met., and for popular comedy shows,

front, across the road, a field of lupins ran wild towards the river bank. Here, one can look across the red mud-flats of the Avon River to the Summerville Shore or out to Minas Basin and the majestic silhouette of Cape Blomidon.

such as "Fibber McGee and Molly." The medium was ideal for government propaganda in aid of the war effort. This was when the local daily farm broadcasts began.

Norm was asked to write the script for a farm-family serial modelled on a programme already started in Ontario. A local legend was born when "The Gillans" came into being; the extended family became so familiar to Maritime listeners that many believed them to be real people. They certainly took over Norm's life. Starting in 1942, for seven and a half years, he wrote five scripts a week, which he sent into Halifax on the train, so that the actors could read their parts live each weekday. In addition to creating believable and interesting characters, Norm had to do all the research for the programme. Every broadcast required extensive inquiry into farm practices, and Norm, who was ever a perfectionist, was in constant contact with local beef, apple and chicken farms and the agricultural experts at the Experimental Farm in Kentville. He sent away for pamphlets and magazines that could add to his knowledge of places, events and country pursuits. Using happenings and conversations in the life of the Gillan family, he was able to pass on numerous helpful wartime recipes and cost-saving tips to the listening public. His fan-mail grew, but, as he later complained, there was no respite. Even when his father died and was lying downstairs in his coffin, Norm was at work. Eventually, the pressure of the daily deadline became too much and he handed the Gillan family and all their friends over to another writer, Kay Hill. He continued his association with the CBC by writing several family serials for CBC International. He also continued to write articles and stories for *Macleans*, *Saturday Night* and *Weekend Magazine*.

1955 to 1962 were Norm's years away from Nova Scotia. He travelled and worked in the United States and Mexico, sending regular letters home to his family and friends that recorded his experiences and impressions of life south of the border, and which were to be kept for future use. When he finally returned home to the old house on Avon Street, he resumed his freelance radio work with his series, "The Rum Runners" and his weekly talks. He soundproofed his room and, with dire threats to his sisters and brother that he was *not* to be interrupted, recorded the pieces on a reel-to-reel tape recorder. He then sent the tapes off to Halifax where they were rebroadcast to his appreciative and devoted audience. The talks that have now been selected for publication come from this collection.

The experience he had gained earlier in writing for "The Gillans," meant that Norm had a marvellous feel for radio. He had a rich and warm voice that instantly commanded attention. His style was personal and conversational, so the listener felt that here was a friend who had just dropped by for a chat. As an aid to reading on radio, Norm developed his own unique style of punctuation that indicated where he would take a breath and which words would be emphasized. The pieces have been slightly edited for this book but the style and tone have been preserved so that Norm's voice can still be heard. In all of them can be found the light touch, happy turn of phrase and wry sense of humour of this master of the spoken word.

This book is affectionately dedicated to Norman Creighton's many friends.

H. J. S., Hantsport, N.S., 1998.

spring

FAREWELL TO WINTER

So we made it! The snow drifts are beginning to disappear and snowdrops are once again in bloom. The days are getting longer, the underwear shorter. No more icy roads; no more antifreeze. Put away the vitamin pills and the cod liver oil. Kick off your overshoes and pack the heavy winter overcoat away in the cedar chest. It's time to straighten up and look around you, and see the world once again.

There's blue up there in the sky, the same as last spring. The brooks are breaking free and flooding their banks. Out on the back lawn, where the snow has melted away, around the big rock maple, there's a hint of colour on the turf. And a whole new green year lies ahead of us; a whole new season, full of beckoning roads, and picnic baskets, swim suits and sunburn, and the tart goodness of an August apple pie.

It's like having a fortune handed to you. Where do you begin? All that sunshine is waiting, vacation projects, canoe trips, the camper you plan to build, scuba div-

ing, trying out the new golf clubs you got at Christmas, or the spinner salmon rod...so many adventures in the months ahead.

I have big things planned for the garden this year. I'm experimenting with some new seeds. I sent all the way to England for them—special varieties of tomatoes, and Brussels sprouts, and peas. They are those little French peas—the sugar peas—so tender you can cook them pods and all. Then there are some new kinds of head lettuce. I can hardly wait for the first salad out of our own garden—with our own lettuce, a sprinkling of parsley, some white raddish, and a few scallions, along with a spoonful of homemade mayonnaise dressing.

But of course spring doesn't really begin until you've picked your first dandelion greens and had them served up along with some fried gaspereau. But that doesn't come for almost a month, towards the end of April.

"...snowdrops are once again in bloom."

In the meantime we can get busy setting up our wine making equipment, to ready ourselves for blackberry time, or blueberry time. This year we might even try some raspberries. If it's anything like the preserved raspberries we put up in bottles last summer it would be a vintage fit for gourmets. A dish of those preserved raspberries was like reliving the golden splendor of an August afternoon. With each spoonful I could see myself out there in the raspberry patch, down by the beehives, the air heady with pollen and the smell of fresh honey, ripening in the comb.

There are so many wonderful things to come in the green growing months ahead, the pear tree you planted two years ago, or the Chinese chestnut, or the Burbank plum.... All winter you've been wondering if perhaps—this spring—they'd be old enough to bloom and bear fruit. Every spring I try to set out three new trees, so each year I have something to look forward to and to dream about while the frost is still on the windowpane.

You know, I've always enjoyed sitting by the fireside of a winter evening, with the wind rattling at the storm door. On those long winter evenings drowsing beside the hearth with a book on your knee, your fancy is weeks away, with the March winds.

How pleasant it is to warm your mind with the thoughts of the bed of tulips you planted

Early spring—from Norm's window.

last fall, the new clump of King Alfred daffodils, the sweet scented jonquils—those tossing shafts of colour and the smell of springtime in the air.

Not that I spend all my time sitting beside the kitchen stove. I love getting outdoors during the winter months, when the air tastes like breathing in wine and you can feel it tingling in your veins. Everything so spotlessly white; the spruce branches outlined with a light powdering of snow....

And what a winter we've had this year, with skating up at the Community Centre, and curling, and parties at New Year. There have been no house flies to bother us, no rose bushes to spray, and no arguments about Daylight Saving Time. There was hot coffee for breakfast....

Oh winter was such a peaceful time, with the enchantment of its street lights, the soft pool of light under each lamp post, the stars over head, and the crunch of snow under your feet...so clean...so quiet. Yes, it's been a good winter. And now it's finished.

Good bye, winter. It was great having you. We never appreciate you until you're all over. Oh well, cheer up friends. Remember: if summer comes, can fall be far behind? ◆

THE TRIALS AND TRIUMPHS
OF CUPID

One of our problems today is that we've grown so cynical that we don't believe anything. We don't even believe in the power of love—in spite of all those greeting cards at the drug store festooned with red roses, and chocolate boxes shaped like a heart. We dismiss these armaments of love as mere commercialism.

But they aren't. They are there to remind us that Cupid, the world's greatest hunter, is as good a marksman as ever. And...he's had some pretty difficult targets.

When Thomas Bryden came out from England, he settled in Pipers Cove, Cape Breton. There he met a girl and fell in love with her. She was of Barra stock and couldn't speak a word of English. Thomas Bryden couldn't understand a word of Gaelic. Yet somehow, they both understood it was love at first sight. They were married, and as the years went by Thomas Bryden picked up a few words of Gaelic and his wife learned to speak English. It turned into one of the happiest marriages in Piper's Cove. Love had found a way and the language barrier disappeared like the snow in spring.

More serious were those feuds among clans themselves, fostered in Scotland many generations before and having no possible relevance to the New World. The way the Macdonalds felt about the Campbells...or the McLeans about the MacLeods....

Picture, then, a little girl at Big Baddeck coming home from school with a friend in tow—a MacLeod—to share a meal. What she hadn't realized was that her parents, who were McLeans from the Island of Muck, disapproved of the MacLeods as a matter of a principle. Of course, the little boy was given a place at the table without one word of question. Highlander hospitality demanded nothing less. However, after the visitor had gone home, the little girl was warned she must never again bring a MacLeod to the house. But as it happens, Cupid turned the tables some years later with a well-placed arrow.

It could have been in retaliation for a defeat Cupid had suffered earlier, on Prince Edward

"...all those greeting cards at the drug store..."

But, for Cupid's greatest victory, we must go to the village of New Annan, in Colchester County. This is the birthplace of Anna Swan who became the largest woman ever born in Nova Scotia. She grew to be seven feet six inches tall and weighed 350 pounds. Even in her teens, she had to eat her meals sitting on the floor with her back to the wall, while the rest of the family sat on chairs round the table. Bumping her head on the door lintel was always a problem and the bed she slept in was far too small.

Phineas T. Barnum, the great American showman who had sponsored the dwarf, Tom Thumb, and brought the Swedish singer, Jenny Lind, to America, negotiated with Anna Swan and her family. For a fee of $1,000 a month she was to appear on exhibition in his New York museum.

It was the beginning of a lucrative career. Soon, Anna Swan began receiving letters from men who said they were madly in love with her, asking for her hand in marriage. Or, did they wish to become her manager and control that $1,000 a month? Anna Swan was not quite so easily duped. She was, as Phineas T. Barnum later wrote: "an intelligent and by no means ill-looking girl." He, too, shared Anna's suspicions about her would-be suitors.

She was now 25, one of Barnum's star attractions. She had money, fame, all the allurements of success. Yet, somehow, it had

Island, where Colonel Thomas Dawson, an ardent Methodist, had left a will that read as follows: "All my children, heirs and successors shall strictly adhere to the church established by Rev. John Wesley and they shall not mix or marry or intermarry with any other denomination. Anyone deviating from this clause shall be excluded from all claim, right, title and their heirs forever." Colonel Dawson lies—significantly—in an unmarked grave in a Protestant Cemetery on University Avenue, Charlottetown.

lost its savour. There was no one with whom she could share all this excitement. When you're a woman seven and a half feet tall—where do you look for a husband?

Joseph Howe put her dilemma in some "Lines Addressed to Anna Swan," that included the following verses:

If Cupid chanced to come this way
He must a long bow draw
(He's just the size of Tom they say)
To hit you in the raw.

Your heart is safe, it beats so high
No lover in the Nation
Could ever hope to waft a sigh
To such an elevation.

The wonderful thing about Anna Swan is that she *did* find Mr. Right. He was another giant like herself, Captain Martin van Buren Bates, of Kentucky—who stood seven feet two and a half inches tall. After their marriage, their careers skyrocketed into one triumphal tour after another and they were received by the royal houses of Europe. They were entertained by the Prince of Wales (later Edward the Seventh), the Grand Duke of Russia, and Prince John of Luxembourg. They

appeared twice before Queen Victoria, who found them utterly charming, and underlined her approval with a number of royal gifts.

Just one thing bothered them though, the rooms everywhere they went were so small... the beds impossible. Captain Bates had such broad shoulders he had to enter a doorway sideways.

So, they decided to retire from show business. They bought a farm in Ohio and here they built a house fit for giants to live in. It was a 17-room house, with ceilings 14 feet high, and doors with a clearance of 8 feet. All the furniture was specially made to order, chairs so big that normal folk had to climb up the rungs to sit on them.

Anna Swan lived to be only 42. In that short life, the girl from New Annan, Colchester County, travelled about the world like royalty, was honoured *by* royalty, but, above everything else, she achieved a happy marriage.

If you'd like to see some of the dresses worn by Anna Swan and the suits worn by her husband, you'll find them in Tatamagouche, N.S., at the Fraser Cultural Centre, Sunrise Trail Museum.

The giantess Anna Swan and her giant husband, Captain Martin van Buren Bates, were surely one of Cupid's most astounding triumphs. ◆

THE SHAMROCK

Tradition has it that Saint Patrick preached a sermon on the Hill of Tara. As he addressed the multitude, he leaned over and picked a sprig of a plant that was growing there—a beautiful green plant with three leaves on the end of a stalk. He used these three leaves to illustrate the doctrine of the Trinity. It is generally supposed that the plant was the shamrock. Ever since then the botanists have been wrangling over what plant it actually was that Saint Patrick picked. The botanists in Ireland say it was one of the clover family, but even they can't agree whether it's *trifolium repens* or *trifolium dublium*. Others claim that it belonged to the oxalis family. No one is sure—except, of course, an Irishman on Saint Patrick's Day. On that day there is no doubt at all because the Irish have been through more than the wordy battles of the botanists. For their forefathers the shamrock was a defiant banner, a ringing declaration of independence. Remember the old song: "they're hanging men and women there for wearin' of the green."

"...a beautiful green plant with three leaves on the end of a stalk..."

Public Gardens, Halifax, N.S.

Even today, after a hundred and fifty years, the descendents of Irish who came to Nova Scotia and Prince Edward Island and New Brunswick still refer to the shamrock as "that precious plant." Yet no one is really sure what it is.

If it is one of the clovers, we probably have the shamrock growing right here in the Maritimes. The creeping white clover is about the most common clover in Ireland, and also in Nova Scotia, and I expect in Prince Edward Island and New Brunswick as well. But what good does it do us? On March 17 you want a sprig of shamrock to wear on your coat, and at this season our clovers are completely dormant and covered with snow.

So we have to fall back on potted house plants, obtained from florists, and these are generally of the *Oxalis* family. But even if we have no shamrock growing here in the Maritimes, the love of Ireland is still kept alive, with plants, and trees, and memories, nourished from generation to generation.

In the Public Gardens in Halifax grows a clump of the plant *ajuga*. It's a creeping plant, with dark purple leaves and blue flowers, used in rock gardens and for border plants—an exceptionally hardy perennial. A root of it could remain out of the ground for weeks and still retain life. Back about a hundred years ago, a young man came out from Ireland to Halifax, and hidden in the lining of his hat was a root of *ajuga*. That man became one of the first gardeners at the Public Gardens and one of the first things he did was to plant this root of *ajuga*, from his cottage garden back home. The plant is still growing there in the Halifax Public Gardens.

Oak trees were brought out from Ireland by Richard John Uniacke, attorney general of Nova Scotia in the early 1800s and planted on his 5,000 acre estate in Mount Uniacke. And incidentally, the name Mount Uniacke itself is an import. The family seat of the Uniackes was at Mount Uniacke in Ireland, in Cork county.

Of course there wasn't much room for oak trees on those old square-riggers that brought the first immigrants to Canada, both from Scotland and Ireland. The hardships suffered on those voyages can only be guessed at. We have some idea from the shipping news of the day.

• July 16, 1819, brig *Mermaid*, from Dublin, with 73 passengers, went ashore near Cape Negro. The vessel was lost, the crew and passengers saved.

• May 13, 1826, the *Nassau*, from Dublin. 140 passengers, wrecked on Sable Island. And that's all it says—probably not one of them saved.

• July, 1827, Irish immigrants arrive in Halifax —with smallpox.

• May, 1828, barque *Granicus*, from Cork, wrecked on Anticosti. Horrible ordeal in the winter. No survivors.

And so it goes, on and on. Only the lucky ones got here.

The other day I was talking to a good friend and neighbour, and something he told me brought those far off days a little closer. His grandmother, who was born in the county Tyrone in northern Ireland in 1823, came out to Canada with her family when she was only twelve years old, and often told the story to her grandchildren. There were many passengers on the ship. On the long voyage out, which sometimes took three months, four babies were born. The ship docked at Saint John. Some of the passengers kept on up the St. John River, but her parents chartered a little coasting schooner, crossed the Bay of Fundy, and came ashore at Morden, near Harbourville, N.S., probably the first settlers in the vicinity of Harbourville.

When she was an old lady of almost 90, she would talk about the place where she was born and grew up. She could remember the stone walls, the stone arches, the stone houses of Ireland. One of her dearest possessions was a Paisley shawl she had worn on that voyage out to the New World so long, long ago. My neighbour still has that Paisley shawl.

With memories like this, still kept green, we shall always know that the plant we wear today is indeed the one that Saint Patrick picked when he preached his sermon on the Hill of Tara.

◆

HOW ST. PATRICK RID PICTOU ISLAND OF SNAKES

Lying off Pictou Harbour, halfway across the Strait from N.S. to P.E.I., is an island, Pictou Island. It is five miles long and about a mile and three-quarters wide. Towards one end the land rises to a height of 150 feet. Much of it is farmland, and good farmland too—a sandy loam. They've raised some fine crops on Pictou Island.

The families living on Pictou Island today are doubtless descendants of the men and women who first cleared this island. McLean, McDonald, McCallum, McKenzie, McFarland, Patterson, Rankin, Campbell, Hoggs, and Curry were the original settlers.

To many of us it seems a lonely life, being six miles off the coast, especially in winter. But Pictou Island has certain charms all its own and one of these is the absence of snakes. There is not a snake on the island—not even a little green grass snake. Like Ireland, Pictou Island is completely free of snakes. You might ask how that came to pass.

It all started in Europe, in the year 400, when the first Christian missionaries came to England. One of these missionaries, named St. Petrox, settled in Cornwall in the south of England. He was amazingly good as an exorcist.

When it came to exorcism, St. Petrox could do just about anything. His specialty was dragons, breathing fire and with or without wings. St. Petrox could tackle any of them, because when he slew a dragon, he knew he

"...this snake has been travelling about the world..."

10

was slaying evil. That is the reason St. Petrox came to England in those very early days when England was still a pagan land—to rid the country of evil and to get rid of all the dragons...and the snakes.

His first trial began in Cornwall where he was thrown into a grotto of snakes. He had come armed with bell, book and candle and when he went into the grotto his exorcisms caused the snakes to devour each other.

They went on devouring each other for over two days; there were a tremendous lot of them. When they had almost got through devouring each other, there were only two left. These snakes had grown to an enormous size because they had all the other snakes inside them. In fact, to get down to the statistics of the thing, each snake was half a mile long. Then one of these snakes swallowed the other and that, of course, made him a mile long. St. Petrox drove the snake out to sea and this mighty creature swam over to Ireland.

Now you can imagine how evil that snake would be—a mile long. He became the King of Serpents and drew to Ireland all the serpents of Northern Europe, even from Scotland and the Hebrides. Ireland was simply overrun with snakes; you could hardly walk anywhere without stepping on one. It was very unsafe.

All this time this great King Serpent was growing bigger and just eating up everything in sight, including all the little snakes.

At this point, word got over to Scotland and reached the ears of one of the most famous men Scotland ever produced, the man who was later to be known as St. Patrick. He crossed over to Ireland, determined to try his powers on this great King Serpent and his host of smaller snakes.

His exorcism succeeded pretty well on the lesser snakes but it took St. Patrick two weeks, (some authorities say three) to move the monster which was coiled up in a cavern near Dublin. At last the saintly rites prevailed. The serpent slowly put forth to sea, and when its head was going out of Cork harbour, its tail was just leaving Dublin.

Since that time, this snake has been travelling about the world and appearing now and then as a sea serpent. He has been seen off the east coast of Prince Edward Island. Several times he was sighted in Saint Margarets Bay. Though he has never been reported in the vicinity of Pictou, he must at one time have become hungry and come ashore on Pictou Island. That is the only explanation I can think of to account for the fact that, like Ireland itself, on Pictou Island there's not a snake to be seen.

◈

MUD—

SPRINGTIME'S CALLING CARD

Now that the March sun is beginning to nibble at the frost and honeycomb the roadside snow drifts, we are starting to dream about what lies under the snow.

Here and there, around the trees first, the garden begins to appear. Already there are snowdrops raising brave spears through a crust of snow. Out back of the garage the snow has melted away to disclose tunnels made by an animal who, for part of the winter, made his home under the building—a muskrat who has been driven up from the brook by the spring freshets. And the dead grass under the snow is worn away by the serpentine pathways of field mice.

I look forward with a special entertainment to when the snow disappears from our primula bed. Last summer I grew some new varieties of Himalayan primulas, and this will be their first summer blooming.

We should really be very happy in this bracing month of March, with the snow giving away to sunshine, and the frost coming out of the ground...and mud beginning to appear on the hall carpet and yet....

"the frost coming out of the ground...and mud beginning to appear..."

Some friends of ours have been supplementing their income by taking in a roomer, and they're beginning to discover that taking roomers is not quite as uncomplicated as it sounds.

Now this roomer works as a bookkeeper. She's a very nice person, has been working all her life, and pays her rent like clockwork every Friday night. Everything was going along fine until the first of March. Then the mud started showing up. This roomer of theirs, you see, has reached the age where it's a trial to have to take off her overshoes before she sits down in her own room. When she comes in, she tramps along the hall over the newly waxed floor, then clumps downstairs leaving a trail of salty mud on the new stair carpet. She doesn't mean to do this; she is quite unaware of it, in

fact. Her eyesight isn't too good, except for close up work like adding up figures and balancing ledgers and things like that. My friends don't like to point out the muddy footsteps. She's so neat, tidy and always pays her rent. It's simply that she doesn't take her overshoes off....

I have another friend who works on the railroad as a section man and he tells me he's been having his troubles now that March is here. His wife won't even let him in the house until he has taken off his overshoes and his overalls and left them in the back porch.

Of course if we think *we* have problems with mud, we should look back to what people *used* to have to put up with. Consider what the ladies in Halifax faced as the March snowbanks shrank back into mud puddles. In the year 1816, according to one report, "the streets had been so much neglected that in many places they were impassable from the accumulation of rubbish and the broken condition of the wooden platform or bridges at the gutters and crossings." Over in Saint John, the mud was so bad that one man used to take

his wife to church in a wheelbarrow so the mud wouldn't soil her Sunday shoes or defile the folds at the bottom of her flowing skirt.

As late as the beginning of this century, wooden sidewalks were quite common in Halifax and Saint John. Only the business districts had sidewalks of bricks or stone, with paving stones laid across the street at intersections so that pedestrians could safely negotiate the muddy streets. Phyllis R. Blakeley, in her sprightly *Glimpses of Halifax*, tells us that, "grocers and butchers often threw rotten apples, sheep heads, and ox-hides in the gutters in front of their stores...." The mud in those days was really pungent.

In 1904, the principal streets in Charlottetown were macadamized and the good red Island mud ceased to be an affliction to Charlottetown housewives.

But as you know, as we look back on this muddy past, we perhaps tend to forget some of the more happy moments associated with the mud of the springtime. Do you remember the games of marbles around the school yard? They never started up until you could scoop out of the mud a sort of billiards pocket at which you aimed. Then there was another game, played with two sticks, which required an indentation in the muddy sidewalk.

Along those sidewalks, strolled the dandies and gentlemen in their spatterdashes—a kind

"...gentlemen in their spatterdashes—a kind of legging or puttee, which offered protection..."

of legging or puttee, which offered protection for their immaculate pant legs—an accessory which later dwindled down into those dapper little grey spats of the 1920's. Girls would hardly give a glance at any man not wearing spats. So you see, men did manage to get some mileage out of the mud in those days.

As for the women, well, it probably led to one of fashion's most daring innovations: a slit up the hobbled-skirt, calf high, to allow her to better manoeuver those muddy crossings.

So let's not fret too much about a little mud in the front hall. It's just springtime's calling card which reminds us that the crocus and tulips will soon be here. ◆

"Do you remember the games of marbles around the school yard?"

SUGAR-MAKING TIME

The Society for the Propagation of the Gospel has its headquarters in England and was founded in 1701, by royal charter. Its missionaries work on every continent, providing for not only the spiritual but also the physical needs of the overseas church.

Consequently, they have gathered a vast amount of information about the health of many of the colonies, including our first Maritimes settlements. Some of this information runs counter to what we have been led to believe.

According to figures provided by a missionary living in New Brunswick in the late 1700s, the early Loyalists were as about as rugged and long-lived a group as you would find anywhere. Even today.

In the year 1800, this missionary reports that he had baptized (in the previous five years) some 295 infants, married 48 couples and buried 17 persons. In the years 1811 and 1812, he baptized 115 infants, married 40 couples, and buried only 8 people. It was a very healthy place to be living—in New

Brunswick, in those early years of settlement.

There are several sound reasons why this should be so. In the first place, many had escaped from the unhealthy conditions of New York and Connecticut, where tainted drinking water and crowding together in pest-ridden towns helped spread the great scourges of the age: typhoid, cholera, smallpox.

In New Brunswick, these fortunate Loyalists found a place where they had room to breathe the purer air. They lived on a diet which, through necessity, was made up of the simplest foods, provided by the work of their own hands.

They learned to supplement their scanty supplies of flour with Indian corn, buckwheat,

Mountain Maple Lodge, Black River, Kings Co., N.S.
"...where you can still buy...direct from the producers..."

rye and oats. Corncakes, buckwheat pancakes, oatmeal porridge, to this day remain staple foods in many New Brunswick homes. They made use of fiddlehead greens, dandelions greens, and even the greens that grew out on the salt marshes—samphire and gooseneck. They harvested cranberries and wild cherries. For something sweet to go on their blueberries and blackberries, the Indians showed them how to tap the maple tree, and make their own syrup and their own sugar.

Today maple syrup is as popular as ever, sought after eagerly as a gourmet item. There's never enough. It's always in short supply, generally unprocurable after the sugar-making season. If you'd like some to go on your pancakes or your waffles, now is the time to lay in a supply. They're actually making maple syrup, right now—in the sugar bush in New Brunswick and Nova Scotia.

One of the virtues of maple syrup (and maple sugar) is that this is one of the few cases where you can still buy a food product direct from the producer, without anyone else meddling with it. Most of our maple syrup is sold to customers who go right to the sugar bush to buy it.

Maple sugar making has never become a big business operation because, for one thing, it's such a complicated, long drawn-out process. It involves tapping trees and gathering the sap (which today is done by plastic tubing running from tree to tree). Then the sap has to be boiled down. This takes much time and attention and many cords of firewood. The amount of sap required is astonishing—

"Today maple syrup is as popular as ever...a gourmet item."

something like ten gallons of sap for one pound of maple sugar.

There's a story they tell at Wittenburg, in Colchester County, N.S., about one of the first grantees at Wittenburg, John Best, who had been induced to leave his native England and come to Canada by tales that this sugar in Canada—maple sugar—came direct from the trees. After he and his wife arrived in Wittenburg, they discovered to their disappointment, that the maple sap had to be boiled for hours and hours before it turned into sugar.

And, by the way, if you're interested in cooking with maple sugar, there are many old traditional recipes you can try. How do these sound? Maple sugar pie, or maple syrup pie, or Backwoods Pie?

Marie Nightingale prefaces the maple recipes in her cookbook, *Out of Old Nova Scotia Kitchens*, with a little verse about sugaring-off time in Cumberland County.

It's April and again I turn a page in memory's book,
And walk again the maple hills and hear a noisy brook,
In Cumberland the miracle of spring is more sublime
Than anywhere in other lands—it's sugar-making time.

Fondly I eye the amber glow of candy on the snow,
No mortal mind can e'er concoct or man's wisdom bestow
A gift so rare to palate's bliss—God holds the recipe
He wrote it just inside the bark of each tall maple tree.

LENT
TODAY AND YESTERDAY

If you happen to live in an Acadian community—like Prince Edward Island's Mt. Carmel, or Abrams Village, or perhaps in Antigonish County, Nova Scotia, at Havre Boucher, but especially if you live in Cape Breton, at Cheticamp—then this is one of the fun times of the year, the season of La Mi-Carême.

You've never heard of *La Mi-Carême*? Well, it's an old Acadian custom which goes back for centuries and is still cherished and kept alive in places like Abram's Village and Cheticamp.

La Mi-Carême simply means the middle of Lent. It's a time for people to relax a bit on their Lenten vows and allow children to have a few sweets—a cookie or two, perhaps a stick of gum—a little indulgence to human frailty.

During this time, especially in Cheticamp, people go about in the evening from house to house dressed up in costumes. The costumes are often frightening, maybe a white sheet,

covering the head so that it screens part of the face, with holes cut out for eyes and mouth. You might mistake them for Hallowe'en goblins, but these bogey men and women don't come to the door asking for treats. They have some treats with them — an apple or candy— to dole out to the children who've been good.

This cheerful fun-filled Acadian custom is not as popular as it used to be, simply because Lent itself has almost become an anachronism. Who keeps Lent today? Dances are still being held. Nobody's giving up candy. Nobody refuses a glass of beer, and nobody is cutting down on calories.

As a Toronto professor puts it, Father Leo Walsh of St. Michael's College, "Individual over-indulgence may not be called gluttony these days...but you could say we're all guilty

---

"La Mi-Carême...means the middle of Lent—a time for people to relax a bit on their Lenten vows..."

of it here in Canada...when 500 million people in the world are starving."

There was something to be said for Lent, you know, as a reminder of how fortunate we were and to make us appreciate the blessing of a hearty appetite.

But with Lent gone, the need for a break in the middle of Lent has quite disappeared. The only people today observing Lent are the Weight Watchers. Everyone else seems to be scurrying off to a new dining spot specializing in stuffed pork tenderloin served with prune sauce, or roast Quebec duckling with sweet blue plums.

It is not like it used to be, when fasting was in fashion, not only during Lent, but in other seasons as well—if the coastal schooner didn't make it in the fall. That was true of many villages along our coast which depended on ships to bring them their winter supplies.

Take a place like Five Islands, off the shore of Minas Basin, not far from Parrsboro, N.S. The vessel could make it to port here only in good weather. So, when fall came, enough food had to be ordered to last till spring.

Before the ice went out in the bay, many things would be in short supply. One item

"...in Cheticamp, people go about...from house to house dressed up in costumes...they have some treats for children who've been good."

they often ran out of was salt—ordinary table salt. But they had a way of dealing with this problem. Locally there were certain springs, known as "salt springs." The householder would fetch some water from the salt springs and boil it down and make his own salt.

If they ran out of yeast, they would go into the forest and, from the bark of the maple tree, obtain a substance they called "cruttle" which apparently could be used in the place of yeast.

They were an ingenious people, the people of Five Islands. But often, too, a fasting people if the vessels didn't get through.

In New Brunswick, during that first winter and spring when the Loyalists were getting settled in, (the winter of 1783-84) supplies were so scarce at Fredericton at one of the main provision centres that they were down to half a box of biscuits.

In the spring, the settlers at Fredericton planted a few potatoes. But before long they were so hungry that they dug up the seed potatoes and ate them.

*"La Mi-Carême...
costumes are often
frightening..."*

During the summer, they had a stroke of luck. They discovered patches of pure white beans that had been planted by the French but were by then growing wild. One of the Fredericton pioneers, Mrs. Fisher, said, "In our joy at the discovery, we called them at first, 'Royal Provincials' bread,' but afterwards we called them 'the staff of life...and the hope of the starving.'"

It is strange to think that the French, expelled only a generation before, had left behind them something that could help support this other flood of refugees who were now being expelled from the United States.

For those gaunt men and women of the past—both French and English—the times had become Lenten indeed. Yet, even then, when there was little enough to give up, there were those who gave up *something* during the 40 days between Ash Wednesday and Easter.

◆

*"You might mistake
them for Hallowe'en
goblins..."*

EASTER AND THE SPIRIT
OF SHARING

Easter, almost more than Christmas, is a time when the spirit of community blooms in our land along with the spring flowers. The Easter Parade is a social phenomenon quite as much as a religious one. After our dull house-bound winter we look forward to getting out and meeting our friends, and sharing things with them.

The Malecite Indians of New Brunswick have a friendly way of celebrating Easter. The Indians of the Tobique Reserve, on the St. John River above Fredericton, hold a picnic on Easter Sunday in the woods. It doesn't matter how cold the day is, or even if it is snowing. They get together out in the woods, among the swelling buds of springtime, to share in mutual hospitality. If Easter happens to come late, one of the dishes they may have at the picnic is fried gaspereau.

For the benefit of those who haven't lived here in the Maritimes very long, I should explain just what these gaspereau are. They're a fish, a relative of the herring. In April and May great schools of them approach the Maritimes in a mating urge that takes them up rivers to fresh water, to spawning grounds.

"...I should explain just what these gaspereau are."
Decorative Fish, acrylic by Elizabeth Sircom

People from far and wide go to these rivers with dip-nets and dip out these blue shimmering fish. One of these rivers in the Annapolis Valley is so famous for them it is named the Gaspereau River, and in some years the fishermen dip them out by the barrelful. Some people find these fish rather bony, but for myself I can't think of a more appropriate springtime meal—especially at Easter—than fried gaspereau along with dandelion greens.

On the street where I live, these gaspereau sometimes pose a bit of a problem at this season of the year. We get along together in a nice, neighbourly fashion; we are a very compact little community; we are all friends, willing to help out in an emergency and that sort of thing. A good deal of sharing goes on. Someone makes a batch of homemade bread and they bake an extra loaf or two. Pretty soon you see them running across the street to their friends with a loaf of this beautiful homemade bread. It goes on all year round. In the summer those who have gardens share cucumbers and cabbages with their friends who don't have a garden. Fall comes along and pretty soon it's pickling time. Then you start getting bottles of dill pickles, and chow-chow, and mustard pickles—the old fashioned home-made kind, done up with wax paper on the top. Well, that's the kind of people they are—real honest-to-goodness neighbours, always running in with something.

Now don't imagine it's a one-sided affair. We run right back with something just as fast as we can, and therein lies the problem. It's a matter of keeping the books balanced, so to speak.

We share other things too—like seeds from our Russell lupins, and cuttings from a cabbage rose. We're all flower gardeners. We have little roots of bleeding hearts we want to get rid of, mallow and sweet William that have run riot in the perennial border, tulip bulbs that have to be separated to make them bloom. After you separate them, what do you do with all the extra bulbs? It's a sin to toss them out into a compost heap. So, we pack a little basket and trot over to the neighbours. Pretty soon they come trotting back with some mallow or sweet William of their own. That's how it works. It's all very fair. Nobody gets ahead of anybody else.

But at times some of us *do* get ahead—for awhile anyway. We steal a march on the neighbors with some especially delicious Parkerhouse rolls, or a few turnips from the root cellar that are still good (but will soon need to be thrown out). We pile up a tidy balance sheet in our favour, and then we sit back and wait for things to come in.

So what about these gaspereau? Well, our street runs along the bank of the river, the Avon River, and many of us have beach properties, which allows us to set out nets—gaspereau nets. Some of us do! When the gaspereau are running a man with a net is the envy of his neighbors, because you couldn't get fish any fresher than this! And the quantities they catch...hundreds of them

on a tide! Some people salt them for use next winter. Others store them in the deep freeze. They have little smokehouses where they smoke them, and these smoked gaspereau are tucked away in the freezer...and then...there comes a time when they can't do anything more. The freezer is packed full. Then they start going about to the neighbours with a basket filled with gaspereau, and they invite everyone to help themselves to just as many as they want. They leave buckets of them on our doorsteps, so that the freezing compartments along our street are soon loaded up with gaspereau.

Of course this gives the man with the gaspereau net a tremendous lead over the rest of us. With a good gaspereau net you can score

"Then they start going about to the neighbours with a basket filled with gaspereau..."

such a staggering credit among the neighbours that you will be kept supplied with pickles, and crabapple jelly, and orange marmalade for months and months.

As a matter of fact...I'm thinking about putting out a gaspereau net myself. So perhaps I shouldn't bring this matter up until next year. After all, it is nice being neighbourly—especially when you have a gaspereau net.

THE PERILS OF HOUSECLEANING

Richard John Uniacke, the Province's Attorney General and the most influential Nova Scotian of his day, died in the autumn of 1830, at his home at Mount Uniacke. This stately mansion is now open to the public and is unique in the fact that it contains the original furnishings of the Uniacke family, including the library of law books.

In addition to these printed books, Uniacke left behind him voluminous records of the early history of Nova Scotia. But today, those records no longer exist.

They do not exist because he happened to have a daughter-in-law whose passion was housecleaning. All summer long she was airing things and superintending the beating of the carpets. Then came fall housecleaning, followed by a lull during the winter months, and made up for by a mighty spring housecleaning. In the spring following her father-in-law's death, she stage-managed the biggest housecleaning they had ever seen in Mount Uniacke. A bonfire was start-

ed and into the flames went all these old documents and papers from Richard John Uniacke's library, along with many notebooks and journals into which he had poured the details and anecdotes of a long life of public service. They'd only be gathering dust, so...the obvious thing was to get rid of them. You just can't allow the house to get cluttered up with a lot of old papers. You can't hold on to everything.

This is fair enough. No one wants to live like Hetty Green, who never threw away anything she had once laid her hands on. But, sometimes, this trash we consign to the backyard incinerator, or put out in the garbage bag, is more than just a winter's accumulation of out-of-date catalogues and bundles of old Christmas cards and last year's calendars. Sometimes, as in that housecleaning

Uniacke House, N.S. "This stately mansion is now open to the public..."

at Mount Uniacke, we get carried away by our enthusiasm to get rid of things. Papers, of course, are notorious for gathering dust... old deeds... account books and...birth certificates and things like that.... So, out they go. In hundreds of homes throughout the Maritimes, our housecleaning fever keeps the fire crackling and with each year, a little more of our history goes up in smoke.

Such irreplaceable documents as a parish register or a ship's passenger list, which could provide the one missing clue in someone's search for their origins in Scotland or Ireland, would be treasured by your local historical society. They would be very happy to make a photocopy of these documents and then return the original to you.

The search for our family history is being pursued more eagerly today then ever before and the job of answering the inquires from Alberta, or B.C., Boston, or California, falls, for the most part, on our local historical societies. They manage to get through an astonishing amount of work, all of it done by volunteers who are anxious to save those priceless records that all too often get tossed out...during our sudden fits of housecleaning.   ◆

"...our housecleaning fever keeps the fire crackling..."

THE GANDER MONTH

In Kings County, Nova Scotia, they used to tell a story, whenever April came around, about someone working on a farm as a hired man who had to quit his job to go and help out on his brother's farm. The farmer where he had been employed would only pay him for two weeks work, but the hired man claimed he'd been there for four weeks.

This hired man had little in the way of an education but he knew his rights and was not giving up those two weeks pay without a fight. So the argument finally ended up in court.

The judge said to him, "You say you've put in four weeks of work already?"

"That's right, your honour."

"Well how am I to know you are telling the truth?"

"Because the goose hatched out the day before I left."

"I don't quite understand. What goose?"

"Well, May, she set the goose the day I left home to go to work and it came off the nest the day before I left my job. So that's 28 days. And that's four weeks."

He won his case because in those days, in a farming community like Kings County, even the judge was aware that a goose takes 28 days to hatch out her eggs.

In fact, farmers refer to April as The Gander Month. Why? The gander is one of nature's most attentive mates. He watches over the goose the entire 28 days while she is sitting on the nest, standing guard over the nest night and day. Sometimes he stands on one leg and then the other. If the goose comes off the nest to get something to eat, then the old gander will take a spell on the nest and keep the eggs warm until she gets back. After the goslings are hatched out, woe betide any human or animal who gets too close to the nest. He'll fight them off with fearsome hisses and great flapping wings, because he's hatching out a

"The gander is one of nature's most attentive mates."

project, a springtime dream of a flock of goslings to waddle proudly after their father. The Gander Month is a time for many dreams.

Last year, in April, our cat had kittens, and now she is due to have kittens again. April seems to be the month for kittens as well as raising tomato plants, chickens and goslings, and starting a new hive of bees. It is a month of beginnings when hope once again takes root across the land.

It is a month of happy endings as well as we pack away in the cedar chest all our thermal underwear, pile-lined jackets, parkas and duffle coats, and kick off our overshoes for the last time, ridding ourselves of 15 pounds of excess weight. When it come to losing weight, no crash diet can compare with these first light-hearted weeks of April.

Speaking of diets, pretty soon we are due for a fresh run of smelts which always happens after the first snow in April. At least that's what they tell me up at the post office, though there are others who maintain that the first snow in April is called the robin snow. (I've never been quite sure which it is; but it's either the robin snow, or the smelt snow.)

Once you have smelts it is only a matter of days before the gaspereau start running. Hundreds of thousands of them are on their annual migration to the spawning grounds at the head of many of our Maritime rivers. We make a big thing about the salmon fighting his way upstream, but the gaspereau do exactly the same thing, and if they were only as scarce as salmon, they would be selling for

$2.00 apiece. As it is, the price is closer to $2.00 a dozen if you are lucky enough to be there by the riverside when they are landing them from the nets.

While on the subject of good things to eat, if you should happen to live down around Yarmouth, you will be having that popular Yarmouth dish, parsnip stew. This is made with chopped onions, browned in the frying pan, some diced potatoes, slices of pork of some kind along with some chopped up parsnips, all simmered slowly together in the stew pot. This is the season for parsnips; right now they are at their very best. Of course, in Yarmouth, they have known that for a long time.

What else can we look forward to? Well, today is the day the cormorants return to Pictou Harbour. At least it is generally on the first of April. Back in 1974 something held them up at their southern wintering grounds and the cormorants did not make it to Pictou until the eighth, but that was unusual. Today you would stand a good chance of seeing an advance guard of this double-crested water bird return to their favorite breeding grounds. They will be on some old pier pilings along the causeway in Pictou Harbor.

Like the gander, they have a few dreams they would like to get underway, and there is no better time for it than the Gander Month.

◆

BETWEEN HAY AND GRASS

There once lived a mighty giant named Antaeus. His father's name was Poseidon, and his mother was the earth. Mother Earth so loved this son of hers, that she vowed that as long as he remained in contact with her he would be invincible. Nothing could kill him. In fact, when the greatest hero Hercules had a fight with him and knocked him down, Antaeus rose up from the earth stronger than ever.

I have a neighbour who swears that she is just like Antaeus, the Greek giant; she is never so well as when she is out working in her garden. So of course the coming of spring is for her a pretty important occasion—as it should be for all of us—for surely we are all children of Mother Earth.

Farmers have a name for this time of year. They call it "between hay and grass," which simply means that the hay loft and the barn linters are now just about empty, but it's too soon to turn the cattle out to pasture. So here they are, caught "between hay and grass." It's the lean time of year—the time when cattle begin to show their ribs—the time of year when we reach for the vitamin bottle.

The best vitamin bottle of all is provided by Mother Earth herself. Even when she enters our homes on our muddy overshoes, she's trying, poor dear soul, to let us know it's time we got out in the garden and started grubbing about among the plants with our bare hands. She is doing her best to help us recover the springy step of summertime, to remind us of the tingle of our first sunburn, and the tart goodness of an August apple pie.

Some people, though, will hardly let her in the house. "For goodness' sake," they say, "will you please take those muddy overshoes off and leave them outside on the verandah, I'm trying to keep this house clean!" You see how difficult it is sometimes for Mother Earth to announce the fact that she's here, waiting with open arms, to give us back our strength.

She does it through the English violet, which is in bloom right now. Under a carpet of paddy green leaves you'll find these most delicate and fragrant spring flowers—the English violet. But...in order to pick them, since they grow so close to the earth, you must kneel down. And that's when you start feeling well again, because, like Antaeus, you're once again in contact with Mother Earth.

She gives us back our strength in so many ways. On a day in April, it is there in every breath we draw: the smell of new buds...of catkins on the sugar maple...of new leaves...and grasses...crocus and blue scilla and snowdrops...the smell of things growing.

My neighbour understands this from having survived a good many winters. She deliberately lays plans back in the autumn, planting beds of daffodils, and winter aconite and paper white narcissus, to tempt her out of doors, even in the drenching April rain. She stands there, looking at them, examining each bloom, and then, noting some crocus or grape hyacinth that has been heaved by the frost, she kneels down and carefully pushes the bulb back into the earth. As she does this, the strength begins to flow in through her fingers.

We don't have to be out in the garden long before we hear the robins, the flickers and the tree swallows. They are all here now, enjoying this honeymoon time of year that lies between hay and grass...before the grass offers any real challenge to our panting uproarous lawn-mower. It is a quiet time of year.

It is a time when elderly men—men who you'd think would know better, men liable to be struck down with lumbago at any moment—will steal out of town and go mayflowering. This of course obliges them to bend over, pull leaves aside, and get down on their

"...the hay loft and the barn linters are now just about empty..."

knees to search on the south side of mossy hummocks, where you find the best mayflowers.

Uptown, at the house on the corner, a forsythia bush is in full bloom. Its branches drip with yellow and this has proven so distracting to motorists that one car has already almost run into the town truck that was parked there, loading winter sweepings from the gutter.

This ferment in the air has quite disorganized Main Street. Our taxi driver adamantly refuses to answer the phone. He's out in the driveway painting his flat-bottomed skiff which he plans to load on his trailer. He'll be off to the lakes before dinner.

Along at the barber shop there's a sign out, "Closed for the afternoon, and all day tomorrow." Around the barber's chair are gathered a panel of customers, deliberating over the relative merits of a Parmacheene Belle, a Black Gnat, or a Silver Doctor.

At the hairdresser's next door appointments are completely off schedule, while our beautician steps out to dig up a root of chives, to give to one of her customers.

These are just symptoms of that wonderful time of year—between hay and grass.

◆

PLANTER'S PUNCH

Some years ago I was stricken with a very curious fever. Medical science has no name for this affliction, yet many people suffer from it—especially at this season of the year. It is caused by a germ, otherwise known as a seed. The victim becomes temporarily unbalanced. It took me years to fight my way back to normal health, and I would like to tell you something of that struggle.

Up to the age of twenty, I had never touched a seed catalogue. I was totally ignorant of the difference between a hydrangea and a hollyhock. One day, some friends offered me a little Jerusalem cherry. I didn't like to refuse, so I took it. Before I knew it, they were offering me a lemon verbena. I took that too, along with some grape hyacinths, and from then on it was just a matter of time before I became an addict.

I sent away, all over the world, for seed catalogues and then I started ordering seeds. At first, I grew just the simple little annuals—nothing beyond a light, dry daisy. Then I became fascinated with the deeper colours—the golden ambers, the tawny reds—flowers that had a little more body. In fact, at that time I started going in for the giant cannas. At any rate, I quickly developed a taste for hardy perennials, and for such things as double petunias.

After awhile I noticed that I wasn't satisfied just ordering commonplace seeds, like an old-fashioned sweet William. They had to be rare and exotic—things like passion flower, and orchids, and lotus. When I got as far as ordering lotus seeds, I realized I was in deep water. Finally, I caught myself sending away for the seeds of a century plant, and I knew I was hopelessly insane.

From then on I lost all control, and plunged from one excess to another—from Scarlett O'Hara morning glories to night blooming moonflowers. I soon found myself down in the gutter—looking for loam for the compost.

"Then I started ordering seeds"

Only those who have struck bottom can know the agonizing soul-searching of the man in the grip of this craving. He tries to keep off the thing; he avoids horticultural shows; he resigns from the garden club. Perhaps he goes along quite normally for several weeks, even a month or two. Then someone at the office offers him some sunflower seeds. But of course he can't take them and eat them in a casual, social way. He has to run right off home and plant the things.

I think faith has a lot to do with overcoming these compulsive habits. For awhile I tried Yoga and it seemed to really help. I didn't plant any seeds for almost a month—just a little transplanting in the perennial border, but nothing on the rocks. And then one day a neighbour invited me in and showed me her philodendron. I made a slip, of course, and one slip like that is all you need to start you off again.

It's not easy, I can tell you, fighting your way out of a thing like this. People come in and sit with you. They feed you dandelion tea, and chickweed sandwiches. They try to talk you out of it. It's no use. It's something you

"...it was just a a matter of time before I became an addict."
Norm in his garden.

have to face up to alone, in the quiet of your own greenhouse. You either go to pot—or you reach a point where you stand up and say, "I've had it. I'm quitting. I've planted my last seed!"

It takes guts. It takes backbone. It takes all the sand and grit you can muster. I suppose the plain fact of the matter is that some of us have more character than others. We can call on inner resources. When the pips are down, when we stand with our backs to the garden wall, it's then that we show what stuff we're really made of.

What's that you're offering me? A Jerusalem cherry! Hm! Brilliant colour. Clear as a crystal. The leaves seem to fairly sparkle. Delightful bouquet. This kind always does so much better at room temperature. Well—there are a thousand reasons why I shouldn't, but I just can't think of one of them. Here's mud in your eye!

OUR EDIBLE WILD PLANTS

Dandelions.

Everyone knows that the lady's slipper stands for Prince Edward Island, that New Brunswick has chosen the purple violet as its official flower, while Nova Scotia's emblem is the mayflower. The mayflower was so designated by special legislation passed in 1901. That legislation was necessary because not everyone wanted the mayflower. There were those who preferred to see another flower elevated to this honour—the dandelion.

And why not? What's wrong with the dandelion? Its cheerful spikes of bloom are heralds of springtime, and back in the 1800s, it had many champions here in Nova Scotia. They used to drink toasts to it. Here is a toast proposed in the year 1814, at the meeting of the English Benevolent Society of Halifax. "The British Constitution: may the rose and thistle, the leek and the shamrock, grow in unison with the dandelion of Nova Scotia and bloom and flourish in spite of all their enemies."

The toast, as far as the dandelion part goes, is as much deserved today as back in 1814, because this vigorous little plant—a weed, some would call it—when used as greens, is more nutritious than virtually any fresh green sold on the market. Dandelion greens contain twice as much vitamin A as spinach, and they're also rich in Vitamin C. Dandelion greens are something you can go out and start gathering right now.

This is the season, as well, for many other edible wild plants which you'll find out in our woodlands, along the seashore, or growing in our ponds and streams.

Don't overlook fiddlehead greens which grow widely in parts of Nova Scotia—both the ostrich fern and the bracken fern. Something else to look for, are the versatile cattails, sometimes mistakenly called bulrushes, familiar plants of wet ditches and marshes. No other plant produces so many kinds of food as the common cattail. If you look among the dried leaves of the previous season, you'll find this year's tender young shoots which taste not unlike cucumber. They can be eaten raw, used in a salad, or, if too mature, the shoots can be boiled in salted water and simmered to tenderness. The cattail's velvet-brown flower heads, which look something like a sausage, can be prepared and eaten like corn on the cob. Some cattail enthusiasts gather the yellow pollen, as fine as sifted flour, to be used in breads, muffins or pancakes.

In fact, a quite nourishing form of flour can be made from the roots of the cattail. Some believe the world's food problems could be largely solved by growing cattails. A yield of 140 tons of roots per acre would produce 32 tons of flour—a much higher yield than you'd get from wheat or any other cereal grains. It's an amazing plant—the cattail, or bulrush.

Only during the past 20 years have we come to appreciate the nutritional value of these wild plants. This is something quite new. Our grandfathers wouldn't have thought of eating such things—and more's the pity. Many people lived on a meager diet during the hungry thirties, when they could have been using these woodland sources to supplement their limited menu. Or consider what the pioneers of this country suffered during those long winters and late springs. They were surrounded on all sides by an abundance of delicacies from the woodlands which they were afraid to eat, because they were things no one had ever tried.

The Mi'kmaq never developed that end-of-winter decline known as scurvy, which is caused by lack of vitamin C. They knew how to get their vitamin C. But of course, who would take advice from the Mi'kmaq? So those hardy pioneers sickened, as the winter wore on and supplies ran short.

Listen to the fate of one of Truro's early settlers, Joel Camp, who, in spite of all that food out there in the forest, quite simply starved to death. It is a tradition around Truro, N.S. that Joel Camp's last meal on this earth was the end of a tallow candle.

An old woman living in Tatamagouche, N.S., in 1831, recalled that, in the spring after she had arrived from Scotland, she and her children went for three months without bread or potatoes, subsisting on shellfish and boiled beach leaves. In Patterson's history of Pictou County, you can read what sparse rations awaited those Highlanders who arrived on the ship *Hector*.

To think that none of that was really necessary! Out there in the forest lands were dozens of wild plants they might have eaten. If only they'd had such a book as *Edible Wild Plants of Nova Scotia* they would have known how to prepare a vitamin rich tea from the young, berryless sprigs of the juniper bush, how to make bread from the inner bark of the pine trees. They would have been aware that the leaves of the poplar tree are edible, tasting much like spinach, that the buds and twigs of the sweet birch are just the thing to nibble on for anyone hiking through the woods.

But even if we, today, don't try these more unusual items, we can all go looking for fiddleheads, and offer a toast to Nova Scotia's unofficial floral emblem—the dandelion.

BLACK BEARS
AND PINK MAYFLOWERS

At a public dinner, held in Halifax in the year 1836, a toast was proposed: "The mayflower—Nova Scotia's emblem. May it's odorous buds, and evergreen leaf never be trodden by the foot of a slave." And I doubt if it ever has been. Searching about for mayflowers, in the shady and snowy retreats of the forest, attracts the free and roving spirit—the bold adventurer—rather than the slave.

Once again, we've reached the season to go mayflowering, to find those dainty emblems of spring, deep rose, and sometimes almost white. If you haven't already thought of going out mayflowering, do consider it for a weekend jaunt.

And now, having urged you to go prowling through the woods, looking for mayflowers, I must warn you that you are in great danger, that your life is in peril. At any moment, you may be attacked by one of the most powerful carnivores of the forest. Because this month of April is when our native black bear emerges from its den after a winter of sleep. If it should happen to be a female, she will have her two romping youngsters, two cute little black bear cubs, to tempt you to get out your camera, and press the button. That is if you enjoy living life dangerously.

Consider the facts. This animal—the only bear we have in the Maritimes—has the habit of walking on the flat of his feet, instead of the toes, as most mammals do. When he stands upright, he is almost as tall as a man, a man who weighs 350 pounds, most of it solid bone and muscle. Our little black bear is an impressive sight when you get close to him. His great

"this month...is when our native black bear emerges from its den..."

*"The mayflower—
Nova Scotia's
emblem."*

strength lies in his forearms and paws. He attacks his prey, not with his teeth, but by striking terrific blows with his fore-paws. If he should ever grab you by his teeth, then be prepared to say good-bye. In those massive jaws are canine teeth and molars strong enough to crush the bones of an ox.

So how do you think you would make out? Run when you see him? Well remember this. He can chalk up to a speed of 30 miles an hour when he wants to. Only a gold medal Olympic sprinter could hope to outrun our native black bear. Fortunately, our black bear is generally running 30 miles an hour in the direction *opposite* to the one you are running.

That's the only thing that saves you: the fact that this mighty creature is extremely shy and secretive and prefers to stay well away from man.

For further reassurance, listen to this letter written from Prince Edward Island, from a place call Maxwelltown, by Walter Johnstone, who had come to the Island from Scotland in 1822, representing the Scottish Missionary Society. He says, "Having mentioned that there are bears upon the Island some will be ready to say we would not like to go to a country where ferocious animals are; we might be torn to pieces by them. Well, I can

assure you, I never had the pleasure or rather the alarm, of seeing one of them alive, after all the solitary journeys I made through the largest woods upon the Island, with no other instrument of self defence but a walking staff. But the truth is, there are a few of them yet in the woods, which are seen occasionally by the inhabitants. And now and then in certain solitary places in the woods, some of the black cattle and sheep are falling a prey to them and the wild cat, while lambs are also occasionally attacked by foxes. But I could never obtain positive evidence that one human being had ever been really killed by the bears upon the Island." That was back in 1822. How about today?

The bear population in Nova Scotia is on the increase, and this is also true, I believe for New Brunswick. They have been increasing because for the past few years they have been protected. Their saving grace is that, normally, they don't want to see any more of us than we want to see them.

If it were not so, the bears and the people searching for mayflowers could never have lived together all these years in this woodsy land of ours. ◆

THE TAKE IT EASY GARDEN

At this season, we're often tempted to plunge into flower gardening. The pictures in the seed catalogues are so gorgeous; Iceland poppies, camelia flowered begonias, flaming zinnias, and golden daylilies, who can resist them? And, as we begin pottering about with a digging fork, we suddenly feel ourselves gloriously in charge of things.

A flower garden offers any one of us the healing balm of mastery and dominion; this is our little principality. Here, among the hot beds and Dutch hoes, we take on the mantle of kingship—ordering our subjects about, re-arranging their lives, even banishing them to the compost heap.

We are led into intoxicating dreams of empire, of sanguinary peony beds, arbours dripping with American Beauties, and peaceful borders humming with spikes of Canterbury bell and foxglove.

And yet, despite all this heady sovereignty, we undergo a strange metamorphosis. The man who would be king is now a servant, toiling among his herbaceous borders, his snap-dragons pouting for water and calling for protection from an icy wind.

It is then I object to growing flowers because the gardener—the deeply-committed gardener—has so little time to enjoy it all. He's too busy lugging things, and laying in an armoury of tools and supplies, spray guns and devastating dusts.

Some years ago I decided there must be an easier way to have a flower garden. The idea came to me while I was out walking on a back road. Some distance from town, I came upon the crumbling foundation of what had been at one time a farmhouse. The house itself was long gone, but clinging to the edge of the foundation was a clump of that old-fashioned foliage plant called trout flower, or sometimes William and Mary, planted lovingly a century or more ago. There were lupins and sweet William and columbine (the old time granny-bonnets). It was a flower garden—a flower garden no one had touched a hoe to in the best part of fifty years.

Consider how little that garden had asked in the way of care and how much pleasure it gave. I returned home wondering if this old foundation didn't provide the answer I was looking for. So I dug up some of these sturdy old flowers and transplanted them into my garden. Friends and neighbours supplied other plants that seemed to look after themselves while remaining immune to disease. One of the best of these, for the early spring garden, is the English violet. English violets, under our Maritime fogs, prosper in the shade of the purple lilac until you have the most fragrant of carpets. Then, for a real ground cover, there's blue periwinkle, and snow-in-summer. They spread without the slightest encouragement.

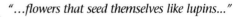

If you like the scent of dried rose petals—the kind our grandmothers made into sachet powders, and stored in potpourris—well, there's really only one kind of rose for this purpose. That is the pillar rose, Maiden's Blush, that has been getting along without cosmetics since the time of Shakespeare. We have a bush in our garden that is over eight feet high. It never winterkills; it needs no attention. It carries a shower of pale pink flowers every July and the dried petals can be stored in a jar and savoured on a wintry evening.

Leave a shady space for some ferns. These can be dug the next time you are out in the woods. You might try your luck with some wild flowers like trillium or Jack-in-the-pulpit but these are more particular and demand just the right growing conditions.

Don't overlook the peony. The peony is one of the hardiest and most persistent of all the perennials. It will come up through heavy sod year after year. We have clumps of peony that haven't been touched in ages and they never fail to bloom.

"...flowers that seed themselves like lupins..."

Peachbells have a way of surviving neglect, likewise the tiny bluebells and bachelor buttons. There are also all those other flowers that seed themselves down like lupins and forget-me-nots. Sometimes they multiply to the point of becoming weeds.

But then what is a weed? A misplaced plant, someone has called it. In my garden, I like to find a place for many of them, along with those early spring bulbs like snowdrops. They tell me, in England, there are fields white with snowdrops.

So now we can sit back in the Cape Cod chair and enjoy the flowers. The big rock maple is beginning to show its pink buds. In a few weeks the cherry tree and the pear will be alive with bees—and the evenings sweet with their May-fresh perfume. The frogs will soon be singing at night. In the mornings, we hear the seagulls crying and across the river the trees are showing the first stirrings of colours.

Our early crocus are putting on a brave display. The patches grow bigger every year, along with winter aconite, and that most heavenly of blue, the scillas. Soon the primulas will be showing, the cowslips, the prim-roses. They have become weeds, gladdening us with their reappearances each spring. No sprays, no insecticides, all we have to do is go out and look at them. That's all they ask...in my take-it-easy flower garden. ◆

A SPRINGTIME BOUQUET

Those of us who live in Canada's Atlantic Provinces are especially sensitive to the advent of Spring—to the sudden brightness of the March sun; the melting snow that still lingers in a ridge between sidewalk and street; the river such a deep blue, with the last of the ice cakes, powdered with fresh snow, floating slowly downstream.

Spring in these parts comes reluctantly. We long for it. To hasten things on, some of us go out into the garden, and into the woods, and cut branches of forsythia and pussy willows and bring them back into the warmth of our kitchens. We watch eagerly each morning as the buds swell and burst into flower, and we almost imagine that Easter has come and gone.

It's no wonder that these Atlantic Provinces produced Canada's springtime poets — Bliss Carman and Charles G. D. Roberts in New Brunswick, Robert Norwood and Kenneth Leslie in Nova Scotia.

I call them springtime poets because so much of their work reflects the joy and wonder of these few precious weeks that lie ahead of us, so unlike any other weeks on any page of the calendar.

Bliss Carman was the first Canadian poet to establish an international reputation. Much of his appeal lay in his haunting mood pieces about the magic of April.

Make me over, Mother April,
When the sap begins to stir!
Fashion me from swamp or meadow,
Garden plot or ferny shadow,
Hyacinth or humble burr.
Make me over, Mother April,
When the sap begins to stir!
Make me over in the morning
From the rag-bag of the world!
Scraps of dream and deeds of daring,
Home-brought stuff from far sea-faring,
Faded colors once so flaring,
Shreds of banners long since furled.
Hues of ash and glints of glory,
In the rag-bag of the world.
Only make me over, April,
When the sap begins to stir!
Make me man or make me woman,
Make me oaf or ape or human,
Cup of flower or cone of fir;
Make me anything but neuter,
When the sap begins to stir!

Our second poet was a cousin of Bliss Carman, Charles G. D. Roberts. In his poetry, too, is the excitement of a world waiting to be re-born.

When winter is done, and April's dawning
Shatters the dark of the year,
And the rain-fed rivulet under the bridge
Again runs clear,
And the shepherd sun comes over the hill
To let out the flocks of Spring,
With laughter and light in the pastures of air
The flocks take wing.

This same delight in things of the earth inspires his "Lines for an Omar Punch-Bowl"—

Omar, dying, left his dust
To the rose and vine in trust.
"Through a thousand springs" —said he,
"Mix your memories with me.
Fire the sap that fills each bud
With an absence from my blood."

Charles G. D. Roberts was for ten years professor of English at King's College in Windsor, N.S., between 1885 and 1895. During those years, a young man from Hubbards Cove enrolled in the theological course. His name was Robert Norwood. Roberts recognized in the young student not only an outstanding gift of oratory but a quite considerable poetic talent. He encouraged him to write.

Robert Norwood was to become one of the greatest orators Canada has ever produced. He was in constant demand as a speaker and travelled throughout the United States and Canada, lecturing with the Chautauqua concert tours, often reading his own poetry.

Here, you find once again this preoccupation with the enchantment of these weeks to come. He says,

Give me a sky of April, blue
As this bit of a broken shell
Found last summer where it fell
Under the robin's nest...

Robert Norwood, although he went on to occupy one of the most impressive pulpits in the United States, at St. Bartholomew's church on Park Avenue in New York City, always remained a Maritimer. Each summer vacation he returned to his old home in Hubbards.

"...They drink the sun to give it back..."

During his later years, he came to enjoy a cordial friendship with our other springtime poet, a much younger man, Kenneth Leslie, who was born in the town of Pictou and lived later on the Magdalen Islands.

In the poetry of Kenneth Leslie is this same reverence for the wonder of rebirth. Here, as our final garland in this springtime bouquet, is Kenneth Leslie's poem "Three Tulips Stand and Talk to Me":

Three tulips stand and talk to me.
One is as yellow as can be,
one red, another purple black.
I hear but cannot answer back;
the things they tell me are so true,
such things there is no answer to.
They say to be a tulip one
must bed in soil, must burn in sun,
must brood in blackness, swell with rain,
must stumble through the earth in pain
from frosty night to flaming song,
to joy that lasts not overlong
in measured time, although they say
no moment ends in tulip day.
To earth they drain their cup of thanks
for broken light in crowded ranks.
They drink the sun to give it back
in yellow, red, and purple black.

◆

summer

SUDDENLY IT'S SUMMER

"Even the old bachelor...is putting up some bird houses..."

Every year it's the same thing. When summer comes I'm never ready for it. You go into the barber shop and somebody says, "Oh yes, there's still snow in the woods. That's where the cool wind is coming from," so you keep on wearing your red plaid woollen jumper. And so does everyone else.

Then suddenly, overnight, summer bursts upon us like a miracle, sending the thermometer soaring into the incredible eighties.

You start off for the post office and you become aware of a new race of people living in this town. They walk differently. Now who's that on ahead? Why, it's the receptionist at the doctor's office, skipping along the sidewalk, now that she's discarded her rain-boots. I had no idea she had such a youthful figure.

Even the old bachelor who lives alone in the tumbled down cottage and hasn't allowed a woman inside his house in years—even he is out this afternoon, moving briskly about in his garden. He's putting up some bird houses, mind you, and hanging out pieces of string, to encourage them in their nest-making.

And here come two young men in shorts and blue blazers. Can these be the charcoal grey financiers in the tellers' wickets who balance up your bank book? Now, they're balancing tennis rackets, and their step is as bouncy as the international exchange rate.

And then there are the girls. These are the true wonder of this time of year. They always take us by surprise, because they certainly weren't here last winter. Not these gay creatures flashing by on their bicycles in beach pullovers and with skirts aswirl. They weren't here. We did have some young people, presumably girls, but they were so bundled up with parkas and scarves, and clumped about in such oversized boots you were never quite certain. But now, like butterflies emerging from a winter cocoon, we have girls, real girls, back with us again. One of them is to be our Apple Blossom Princess—and perhaps even the Apple Blossom Queen for the whole of the Annapolis Valley!

But they really couldn't have a setting more worthy of a Princess than Main Street, with its lawns being mowed for the first time, and at the drug store a window display of suntan lotion and summer perfumes. Along the street, the trees give off their own perfume of budding leaves, and bark in which the sap is running.

How pleasant it is to see these girls pedalling along Main Street, and to know we'll have them with us again for almost five months.

Now they're stopping in front of Don's Restaurant. And by a strange coincidence, the two bank clerks are turning in at the restaurant too. No, no, they're just standing there talking to our Apple Blossom Princess and her friend in the Tattersall check slims. Now they're moving off together, the boys wheeling the bicycles, on their way to the Community Centre. Perhaps the swimming pool is open already. Or perhaps they're planning to take in the Community Centre barn dance tonight.

Whatever it is, these will be days they will always remember. Our season of summer enchantment has begun.

◆

Community Centre,
Churchill House,
Hantsport, N.S.

ARBOR DAY AND
PIONEER ECOLOGIST, TITUS SMITH

Nova Scotia's first settlers established themselves in the shelter of its coves and river valleys, seldom venturing into the interior. Some regarded the forest with horror. They burned it down as opportunity offered. Beasts and bogles haunted the darkness; Indians lurked behind every tree. The forest, the interior forest, was unknown country until 1801.

In that year, the governor of Nova Scotia, Sir John Wentworth, felt it was quite time the province had a reliable map of the hinterland, together with a report on its soil and timber resources. He knew just the person to undertake this exploration—a young man named Titus Smith, farmer by occupation, by profession a land surveyor, by inclination a student of natural history, or as we would say today, of science.

Already Titus Smith had made a name for himself as a botanist; he had also acquired a solid background in biology, chemistry, and geology. To this land-use survey of Nova Scotia's forest lands he brought an observant eye, along with a mind equipped to interpret what he saw. His careful report, now in our Public Archives, has won him recognition as one of the earliest of North American ecologists.

Titus Smith, in his quiet, cheerful way, was something of a maverick. He belonged to a religious sect which did not sanction a paid clergy, and cautioned its members: "If it be possible, as much as in you lies, live peaceably with all men."

George Washington encountered this pacifist spirit during the Revolution when he asked Smith's New England father, who had a considerable knowledge of chemistry, to make gunpowder for the rebel army. The elder Smith refused to do so. He and his family joined the Loyalists and came down to Halifax.

Young Titus was animated with this same independent thinking as he approached his tour of the province's interior wilderness. He meant to follow his own conscience and record the facts, as opposed to the myths.

One fact soon became apparent—the heavy hand of the new settlers, which revealed itself in destruction not only of the forest (largely by fire), but of animals (overhunting), and of man himself (the vanishing Mi'kmaq).

The Mi'kmaq, for some reason, held no terrors for Titus. He wished to get in touch with them and learn what he could of their way of life, but they remained shy and elusive.

On August 27, 1801, near the Nictaux River in Annapolis County, he makes this entry in his notebook:

Saw very frequently this day very old blazed paths of the Indians. Heard some guns near and saw the tracks of Indians but did not find their camp.

Later on he records that the beaver and moose are almost all destroyed in most parts of the province. The caribou are more numerous than the moose but have suffered from the fires which have burnt over the open barrens destroying the white reindeer moss which is their chief food.

Titus Smith explained in detail just what these fires were doing—fires which would one day turn one-fourth of Nova Scotia's forest land into barren heath:

The great influx of inhabitants in 1783 produced a complete change in the forest. The fires necessary for clearing the land were communicated to the spruce thickets. The profusion of herbage which followed, for a time furnished pasture. This failed in three or four years. The next dry season the forest was rekindled, for renewing it, which it would do in a less degree till, the combustible matter being consumed, with the exception of that portion washed by rains into the swamps, the ground becomes so much exhausted, it produces only a growth of healthy shrubs, among which the kalmia predominates.

"...Titus Smith, farmer... land surveyor...student of Natural History..."

Smith's walks through the wilderness—for they were conducted entirely on foot—were taken during the field seasons of 1801 and 1802. He was paid at the rate of 11 shillings and sixpence a day, and on many days he earned every penny of it:

We have been for several days obliged to travel when it rained the whole time; and we are much more liable to turn out of our course than when we have the sun to guide us. In some places we have been obliged to cross burnt barrens where the original growth of spruce had fallen within 3 feet of the ground, crossing each other every way, and a thick growth of young bushes had sprung up. In such places we could form but an indifferent judgment of the distance we travelled as we probably walked more than two miles to advance one. We never had more fatiguing days' journies than those in which we travelled the least distance.

Smith spent more than 150 days in the woods. Some of his time was taken up in constructing rafts on which he crossed the St. Marys River, the Medway, the Mersey, and explored part of Lake Rossignol.

He had time, too, to pick up some local colour along the way. In the vicinity of Shelburne he investigated a mineral spring which—*as I am informed by numbers of people, has effected several cures of old sores, particularly sore legs of some years standing. The spring boils from the Bottom and probably from a considerable depth. The water frequently bursts bottles when they are close corked.*

Near the Tuskets he writes:

There is a French Village below here where the People live entirely upon Eels & Potatoes. One of the most able of them assured me that most of the French Families did not use 4 Pounds of Flour in a year. They keep Sheep enough to make their own Clothing, & the Meat and Butter which they sell supplies them with the little money they need.

From these tours of the interior Titus Smith produced a map which remained the only reliable general map of Nova Scotia until 1835. He also provided a report on the province's timber stands, together with flora lists identifying 33 species of forest trees, 55 shrubs, 20 species of grasses, sedges, and rushes, and 100 kinds of medicinal plants.

His knowledge and use of these medicinal plants was often called on by his neighbours who, it was said, survived one of the cholera epidemics in Halifax due to his instructions.

He lived for another half century, much of it engaged in promoting, with his friend John Young, the study of scientific agriculture. In his later years he moved to a farm in the little hamlet of Dutch Village, on the rural outskirts of Halifax. Because of his wide erudition and benign nature he became known as The Dutch Village Philosopher.

He had one request to make when he died—that he be buried among a grove of birch and pine trees near his farm at Dutch Village. There remains a grey granite obelisk inscribed with these words:

Titus Smith

Died Jan. 4, 1850

Aged 81 yrs.

Today, the trees are gone—so are the lady's-slippers and trillium, the partridge berries and starflowers that once clustered about his grave. Dutch Village is now within city limits; tarmac and split-levels have spread over the fields where he carried on experiments with imported grains and where he introduced rare species of ornamental trees, and flowers such as the frail white bloodroot and the aromatic American spikenard.

But he would be happy to know that his memory is being kept green in our celebration of Arbor Day. If he could tell us but one thing it would surely be to plant trees—and not heedlessly destroy them.

◆

Cartographer's protractor used by Titus Smith.

THE MAN WHO GAVE US APPLE BLOSSOM SUNDAY

Anyone who visits Cavendish, P.E.I. and approaches the rolling lawns of Green Gables sees something more than a green-shuttered house. He sees a vision of Anne, and inside, pecking away at an old-fashioned typewriter, her creator, L. M. Montgomery.

Those who visit the Perkins House in Liverpool, Nova Scotia are made aware of Simeon Perkins, merchant, magistrate, and diarist, who talked the American privateers out of storming the little fort at Liverpool by an exchange of prisoners, a barrel of biscuits, and some rum.

So it is with all the other historic houses throughout the Maritimes; each one reflects the personality of the man or woman who once made this house a home. In Nova Scotia, the Haliburton House at Windsor was the home of the creator of Sam Slick. The Lawrence House at Maitland was the home of W. D. Lawrence, who planned and built Canada's biggest wind ship. Now, it seems, we are to be allowed to visit the Prescott House at Starrs Point, not far from Wolfville.

So—let's see if we can find out who it was who lived in Prescott house, and why we have

honoured him by making his home a museum.

But first, let's take a stroll around these spacious lawns, along the winding paths, under the tall elms, over to these apple trees. You've heard of the Granvenstein apple. Well, the Granvenstein apple was introduced into Nova Scotia's Annapolis Valley by Charles Prescott. And this tree we're looking at once formed part of his extensive orchards. He introduced other apple varieties into the Valley. Northern Spy, Ribston, Baldwin were all first grown here at Starrs Point on the country estate of Charles Prescott.

Now some people, when they discover something good—something profitable—hug it to themselves and refuse to share it with others, but Charles Prescott was not that kind of man. He liked seeing things grow, whether it was on his own farm or his neighbour's farm. So he urged his neighbours to come and help themselves to scions for grafting in the springtime. He made his knowledge of grafting and growing fruit trees available to everyone, without charge. He was, in fact, the Valley's Johnny Appleseed.

As the years passed, and Charles Prescott grew to be a very old man (he died at the age of 87), he had the satisfaction of seeing these

Prescott House at Starrs Point, N.S. "...took 11 years to build, from 1799 to 1810..."

apple orchards spread to every corner of Kings County and down the Valley until finally he had created a new holiday—Apple Blossom Sunday—when people came from far and wide to view the wonder of a whole countryside transformed into a garden, heady with perfume.

He did it all by sharing things with others. That is why he is remembered. Charles Prescott shared many horticultural novelties with his neighbours. He was the first man in Nova Scotia to grow dahlias, he imported pear trees from France, he tested out new varieties of wheat, he built a greenhouse, the first in the Valley, where he grew grapes and melons. All these things he made available to anyone who, like himself, enjoyed watching things grow.

He was always inviting people to the house, to share a meal, to stop overnight, or stay the week. For that kind of hospitality you needed a house with lots and lots of bedrooms, and that's exactly the kind of house Charles

Prescott built for himself, there at Starrs Point, within sight of Cape Blomidon. It took 11 years to build, from 1799 to 1810, out of bricks made right there on the property.

The front door has a big brass key, 12 inches long, there are seven open fireplaces, and one of them has a wine closet set in the chimney for preparing mulled wine. No wonder people liked to visit him. No wonder two of the province's early governors, the Earl of Dalhousie and Sir James Kempt, came there to admire the apple trees and stayed on for days and days, sampling the older kegs of cider.

Now old houses like this, the scene of cheerful banqueting and open-handed hospitality, sometimes have an unhappy end. For awhile it looked as if this might be the fate of the Prescott House. After Charles Prescott's death in 1859, the property went out of the hands of the family, and gradually deteriorated.

Then, in 1930, it was bought by his grand-daughter, Miss Mary Prescott. From then on Miss Prescott and her two sisters made it their home, and for the next 40 years they dedi-cat-ed themselves to restoring the house and grounds and reacquiring the original furnish-ings. Today, when you visit this old Georgian mansion in the heart of Kings County, you get the feel of what it was like to be a country gentleman—a real country gentleman, like Charles Ramage Prescott—the man who gave us Apple Blossom Sunday. ◆

MARSH GREENS

When snowbanks gather in the raspberry patch, when the bare branches of the lilacs thrash against the frosted window-pane and seagulls sweep inland and roost on the chimneys to keep warm, it's then that I see the summer clouds brushing their shadows across the dykelands at Grand Pré and Tantramar. I see the salt marshes adrift with sea lavender and I dream of a most wondrous plant that grows on those misty flats, a plant that is sometimes eaten...delicious...pungent...elusive...the marsh greens.

Did you ever taste marsh greens? I know they're utterly delectable. Everyone tells me they are. I'm very fond of thinking about them, and planning that some day—next summer—I'll go out on the flats and pick some of these greens that are *so* typically Maritime that very few Maritimers have ever eaten them.

When we first came to live in the Annapolis Valley, when I was a boy, one of the first things people told us about was the marsh greens...these savoury wildlings that

"I dream of a most wondrous plant...the marsh greens."

grow out there on the mud flats, free for the taking. So Mother decided we must try them without delay. It was the right season, mid-summer. We went out on the marshes and filled our baskets to overflowing. Triumphantly we carried them home. When dinner was served and Mother helped us all to a heaping spoonful of marsh greens,

"We went out on the marshes and filled our baskets..."

tastes like—oh, it's pretty hard to describe. They have a taste all their own."

"Pretty nice, eh?"

"Oh, it's a gourmet's delight. Folks down in New York would go wild over them, if they knew about them. But of course, it's only people around here who

we ate them and all agreed that they tasted just as you would expect them to taste...like grass that had been soaked in salt water. That was the last time we had marsh greens.

Could we have gathered the wrong thing or did we have uneducated palates? Since then, through the years, every summer I keep hearing about marsh greens. When the last of the hay fields have been mowed, there's always someone who gets a faraway look in his eye and says, "Well, it's time for marsh greens. Ever taste them?"

"No," I try to lie gracefully, "I don't think I have." The truth wouldn't be any fun here.

"You've never tasted marsh greens!"

"No."

"Well, you've certainly been missing a treat!"

"Are they good?" It's a question you just have to ask.

"Are they good? Marsh greens? Why it's one of the most delicate things you ever tasted. It

know where to find them. You just don't pick anything, you know. You have to go to the right places. There's a place up at the inner reaches of Ox-Bow Creek. It's a little hard to find unless you have someone to show you. You can pick beautiful greens there."

I never try to ferret out exactly where the greens are. That wouldn't be cricket. You're supposed to find these wild things yourself. There's a sort of unwritten law that you conspire with nature to protect such delicacies from the heavy pillaging hand of man. You just keep them for yourself.

Last summer this man I'm speaking of lent me a book that explains all about marsh greens. It is a cookbook called *New Brunswick Recipes*, a collection of traditional New Brunswick dishes, complied by the New Brunswick Home Economics Association. These recipes come from all over the province, and make up a big 170-page cookbook of some 20 different chapters. Oh, there are some marvellous things here and some of the dishes are very unusual. Just imagine this now: maple syrup cake, potato fudge, New Brunswick blueberry pancakes served with maple syrup and country sausage. Just think of that. Then there are New Brunswick hamburgers, made with cooked ham, celery, sweet pickle, chopped onion, and two hard-boiled eggs. How about North Shore oyster stew, old-time New Brunswick vegetable soup, or green gooseberry jam? When it comes to potatoes, they have yellow jacket potatoes, potato puff with bacon and tomatoes, and golden baked potatoes (they've been dipped in melted butter and bacon fat and then rolled in crushed corn flakes). These are only a few of the fabulous recipes gathered together in this wonderful cookbook.

Marsh greens? Oh, yes—yes, the marsh greens.... Here is what it says about marsh greens. It seems there are two types of these. One is called samphire...and the other goose tongue greens. "These are famous Albert County greens and grow on the salty marshes of the Petitcodiac. They mature in late July and early August and many an ex-Maritimer plans his or her vacation for that season—just to savour the flavour once more."

There is a nice little picture showing what they look like. The samphire is in a cluster-like form while the goose tongue is like long blades of heavy grass. The instructions are to wash them well and cook in unsalted water until tender, or add them to a piece of boiling pork for the last hour of cooking. (Doesn't that sound good?)

After I had glanced through this cookbook I returned it to my friend and said to him, "Well, how were the greens?"

He looked puzzled. "What greens?"

"The marsh greens you were telling me about."

"Oh, the marsh greens. Yes, well I haven't had a chance to get down to the flats yet. I have a special pair of rubber boots I use for going down on the marsh, it's so muddy.... As soon as I find my boots, I'm going down to the marshlands to pick a basketful. Summer wouldn't be summer without some marsh greens." But somehow, he never does find those rubber boots. And next summer we go through the whole thing all over again.

The greens themselves remain an elusive delight, receding into the misty, fog-shrouded marshlands, forever beckoning. So every year I have this little project in the back of my mind—that this summer I am going to have some marsh greens. As the years roll by, and I still don't get them, they begin to taste better and better.

BEEKEEPING

When sugar was only eight cents a pound visitors used to say to me, "Oh, I see you keep bees. How nice. They must be very fascinating, I'm sure." Then they patted back a yawn as they braced themselves for the expected 20-minute lecture on the life of the bee.

But when the price of sugar soared up to 80 cents a pound, an evil glint came in their eye as they watched me taking the honeycomb from the hive. "Well, "they said, "*you've* found a way to beat this sugar racket! How much honey do you get? Does it really pay you to keep those babies?"

Now, more than ever, people are thinking about setting themselves up with a hive of bees. Is it a good idea? It's hard to say.

I've kept bees for most of my life. I still keep them. I like them—even though at times they don't like me. Summer wouldn't seem like summer without the hum of bees around that little white box out under the cherry tree with its sweet scent of pollen and the heady perfume of ripening honey.

On the face of it, a hive of bees would seem like a good investment for any household with a back yard. It always was a good idea if you liked honey. Bees don't require a great deal of attention. You can go for weeks, even months, without bothering to look at them and all the while these tireless gatherers of nectar and pollen are driving hard at it from dawn to dusk, making honey for you. It takes 300 bees three weeks to gather a pound of honey while you do nothing but sit under a shady tree, sipping a cool beer.

Sounds like your kind of thing? Then why isn't everyone keeping a hive of bees?

The main reason is that bees can sting and on occasion sting so severely that the victim is left with a face swollen up so he can hardly see out of one eye.

There's a mistaken notion that bees get to know their keeper and establish friendly relations with him. Such is not the case; the beekeeper means nothing to them. The reason beekeepers can manage bees without getting stung is that they know how to handle them. They know the signs that warn them to keep away, that it's not the right day, or the right hour, to approach a hive. Beekeepers never step in front of a hive. They always stand to one side. This is so that the bees coming in from a flight don't find the entrance to the hive obstructed. That can be very annoying to the industrious bee, who can't bear to waste a moment.

So to keep free of stings, you simply avoid doing anything that bees find upsetting. You don't crush them or handle them roughly. You don't approach them early in the morning or in the evening, but always during the middle of the day when they're busy gathering nectar. Even if you do get stung it may not be that bad. Most beekeepers grow immune to bee stings. It still hurts, being stung, but anyone who's been keeping bees for a year or so doesn't react to the poison so violently. A tolerance for it is built up.

In fact, I've known beekeepers who deliberately provoke the bees into stinging them because they claimed it cured their arthritis which can be a much more intense pain than any bee sting. One man used to keep a hive of bees in his greenhouse during the winter so that he would have a handy supply of bee venom when his arthritis started acting up during the cold months.

However, most people don't keep bees in order to get stung but to supply them with honey, a product which has had many claims made for it as an aid to health.

Like anything else, of course, it can be overdone. We don't have to go as far as the man who burst into poetry on the virtues of honey in this little verse...

I eat my peas with honey,
I've done it all my life.
It makes the peas taste funny,
But it keeps them on my knife.

" There's a mistaken notion that bees get to know their keeper and establish friendly relations with him. Such is not the case..."

The very fact that honey is sticky has probably kept more people from using it than anything else. They don't like a dribble getting on the tablecloth, yet it's this very stickiness that makes it so effective medicin- ally. Because of its stickiness, it has the power to absorb moisture from anything that comes into contact with it, and as a result kills many virulent germs. That is why cough medicines are so often made with a base of honey. It's said to be an anti- septic strong enough to kill all micro-organisms introduced into it.

When you use honey, you know you're not using anything new or unproved or experi- mental. Honey has been part of man's diet since earliest times. A cave stone-painting from the neolithic age shows that about 15,000 years ago men were gathering honeycombs for food, the same as we do today. In one of the Egyptian pyramids they found some honey that was still usable—that still tasted like honey. It was 3,000 years old!

This traditional sweetener has had some dis- tinguished advocates, including Sir Edmund

"...you can go for weeks even months without bothering to look at them..."

Hilary who led the successful attack on Mt. Everest. Honey was an impor- tant part of the rations used on that expedition. It was also part of the supplies of Sir Francis Chichester, the man who sailed a yacht, solo, across from England to America in record time. During the last Olympic Games honey was eaten by every gold medalist.

Now if you should be thinking of taking up beekeeping—if only one hive, for your own use—you still have time enough to get started this season. Here's what you do. Write to your provincial Department of Agriculture, addressing the letter to the Provincial Apiculturist, which simply means the provincial beekeeper, the man in charge of beekeeping throughout the province. He will advise you what to do, where to obtain your hive and your bees.

The best thing is that these workers never go on strike.

◆

A JUNE WEDDING

It's pretty hard to imagine anything happier than a June wedding, with the red and yellow tulips craning their necks to catch a sight of the bride, and the front lawn all newly mowed, looking as green as the best man. Here's the bride's mother, and the bride herself, in a full length veil with deep lace edging, and a tiara headpiece supporting real flowers, white flowers garnished with a little spray of green leaf. Instead of a choir, we have the soaring roundelays of a pair of song sparrows who built their nest in a honeysuckle vine on the other side of the garage. Everyone is standing out there on the lawn, smiling, waiting for the pictures to be taken. You just can't beat a June wedding.

In this case I happen to know both the bride and the fortunate young man (and the bridesmaid as well) and though it's all turned out so happily, there were a few anxious moments along the way. Perhaps I shouldn't mention this, but for one thing, the groom almost backed out at the last minute.

It happened like this. The night before the wedding, halfway through supper, I received a phone call. It was the groom. He said, "Look, tell me, what is this business about a toast to the bride?"

I said, "What about it?"

He said, "Do I have to get up and make a speech?"

"You have to answer the toast to the bride, yes."

"Well, what do I say?"

"You just say...a few words. These toasts to the bride aren't big long speeches. It's usually something short and funny, you know."

"Short and funny?"

"Yeah."

"Well, that's fine for him, making it short and funny, but what about me? I have to answer it!"

"It's not necessary to make a great big...."

"And all these jokes he's going to tell! How do I know what he's going to say? How am I going to...."

"Now, now, don't get excited."

"I don't know any good jokes. Look, if I have to make up a speech, right there on the spot, I—I'm not going through with this. We'll just have to call it off, that's all, because I...."

"Now hold on. Take it easy. All you have to do is say thank you."

"You said...I'm supposed to make a speech."

"You just say thank you."

"You're sure?"

"...it worked out very happily..."
Photographed at Norm's garden shed.

"Yep. Make it short, see? They like short speeches at weddings. Two words: thank you. Okay?"

"Well, if...if you think that's long enough."

"Don't say another word. I'm going over to see the bride right now. I'll tell her."

So I went over to the home of the bride and found her having supper: a slice of dry Melba toast, one celery stick and a cup of black coffee, unsweetened. She explained, "There is nothing worse than a fat bride. It is absolutely horrible to see a fat bride, so I've been starving myself for the past week."

"Well don't overdo it," I said.

"How do my arms look? Are they too dimpled at the elbow?"

"Your elbows are adorable."

"Because I'm planning to wear lace sleeves."

"Your arms are positively beautiful. Now will you please eat something? Let me raid the refrigerator and get you something substantial."

"Oh, don't open the refrigerator! It's so full now something's liable to fall out. There is all the stuff for the wedding breakfast. I can hardly wait. There's not even room for my bouquet, and it really should be in the fridge to keep it fresh until tomorrow."

"Well, suppose I take it over to the home of the bridesmaid, they should have room in their fridge for your bouquet."

So I took the bride's bouquet over to the home of the bridesmaid, and I found her almost in tears. She'd been reading Kate Aiken's *Book of Etiquette.*

She said, "Now I'm all mixed up, I don't know *what* I'm supposed to do. I wish I'd never read this book."

"Listen," I said, "it's very simple. You come up the aisle. You step to one side to leave room for the bride, and when it reaches the ring ceremony, she will hand you her bouquet. All you have to do is hold her bouquet while the ring ceremony is taking place. Nothing to it."

"But I'm already holding my own bouquet."

"Lay it down on the pew."

"Mm...but I'm also holding the ring for the groom. This is to be a double ring ceremony, you see, and I have to have the ring ready to hand to the bride at the right moment, so she can put it on the groom's finger. How am I going to hold onto two bouquets and look after the ring for the groom?"

"Look, all you need to remember is that you hold on to the groom's ring and the bride's bouquet. When they need them they'll let you know. Then you go into the vestry and sign the book and that's all there is to it. Except...I have been asked to give you strict instructions that you are not to tell a *soul* where they are going for their honeymoon... and you are to see to it that no one ties tin cans on the back of their car, or writes 'Just Married' with red lipstick across the back window...or gets into the bride's suitcase and ties her pyjamas all up in knots. Oh, there's one other thing. If the guests start clinking their glasses and tapping their glasses with a spoon (to encourage the groom to kiss the bride) watch out it doesn't go on for 15 minutes the way it did at the last wedding. She's wearing pearly blush makeup and it can't stand all that much kissing. And she hopes you spread the word that she's collecting pin wheel crystal. Now that's all you need to know. So close up the book of etiquette, and put this bouquet away in your refrigerator, and please don't spill any milk on it."

Well, as I said, it all worked out very happily, as June weddings always do. But there are bound to be these little problems beforehand. It wouldn't be a wedding without them.

As it turned out, the guests did clink their glasses and tap them with a spoon for the best part of 20 minutes. Her pearly blush makeup was completely ruined.

BEAR RIVER AND
ITS CHERRY CARNIVAL

At this time of year, hundreds of motorists make their way to Nova Scotia's Annapolis Valley, to take part in the traditional Cherry Carnival at Bear River, near Digby.

This carnival has been an annual event now for the best part of half a century. And no wonder, the big red Oxhearts and Black Tararians have been grown at Bear River since the place was first settled—even perhaps since the time of Louis Hébert, after whom it is thought Bear River gets its name. That goes back to the days of the Habitation at Port Royal, in the 1600s, when Louis Hebért, our first apothecary and grower of healing roots and herbs, did some exploring up the

Bear River. He was so impressed by the dramatic, hilly country, sloping down to the river, the warm sheltered valley, that he began experimenting there in the growing of grape vines. (Wild grapes found today near Bear River are thought to be descended from those vines set out by Louis Hébert.) And who is to say he didn't set out some cherry trees as well.

Dear knows, it may have been the cherry trees that started all that trouble between the French and the English, because this tangy fruit, with its intoxicating juice, has a strange power to inflame the passions like no other fruit on earth. Nobody gets excited about apples. I never heard of a pear tree being

"...you have plenty of cherries for everyone..."

raided. Even plums, however toothsome, are seldom molested. But the cherry tree...that's something else.

In cherry time, a midsummer madness comes upon us, an intoxication of the blood that cries out for cherry juice. Cherry addicts drive for miles and miles and miles, looking for a likely tree.

The birds, too, descend on the hapless cherry in squawking hordes. A neighbour of mine has a fine old sweet cherry tree alongside his driveway but he is thinking now of cutting it down. The birds don't allow him to sleep in on Sunday mornings. At peep of dawn they're out there in the tree, stuffing themselves and screeching encouragement to their young.

Birds aren't the only raiders of cherry trees. In my home town we have a short street named Cherry Lane, built around a row of cherry trees planted there many years ago, before it was a street. Of course the kids hardly allow the fruit to ripen before they're scrambling up to the topmost branches, breaking off leaves and branches, tossing green cherries and cherry pits onto the pavement. Perhaps twice a day the housewife has to come out and sweep up the street. So the town has suggested cutting the trees down, but the residents of Cherry Lane won't hear of it. After all, how can you live on Cherry Lane if there are no cherry trees? The town pointed out that they get in the way of the snow plough during the winter. Perhaps they do but they also continue to provide us with a springtime hung with

snow from every bough and a summertime treat for the kids.

Now, in Bear River, they solved this problem long ago by making sure that just about every resident has at least one cherry tree, and some a great many, a regular orchard of them. So why should the kids bother raiding a cherry tree?

As for the birds, there are so many cherry trees in Bear River that they've soon had a feast and fly away to try something else. Besides, with large plantations of cherry trees, some of the seeds are bound to germinate and provide wildlings. You'll get wild cherries growing in the nearby woods and I've noticed the birds seem to prefer these wild cherries to the cultivated ones.

So here you have plenty of cherries for everyone. The trees are respected and allowed to mature their fruit until the day of the carnival.

Then, cherry-fanciers from far and near head for Bear River for the Cherry Carnival

"Bear River is beautiful...stand on the bridge which connects the two sections of the town..."

and, as they say, "buy a tree." A whole family will make a day of it with the picnic baskets under the cherry tree, stripping the big Oxhearts and crisp Whitehearts.

From the side of the hills one looks down at the reflections in the river, the cherry orchards themselves, the houses with their European air, with sharply-gabled roofs and verandahs running along the level of the second-floor windows.

Bear River is beautiful enough in the daytime. It's even more attractive at night. Stand on the bridge which connects the two sections of the town and, after dark, look around at the surrounding hills with the twinkling lights of the houses. Listen to the water rippling under the bridge and the voices of people talking. They are sitting out on their side-hill verandahs...and helping themselves to some of those cherries.

◆

*Editor's Note: The Bear River Cherry Carnival has taken place every year since 1893.

"...cherry-fanciers from far and near head for Bear River for the Cherry Carnival..."

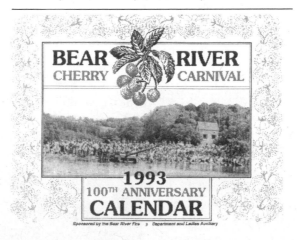

PIGEONS, RAZORBILLS AND OTHER WINGED WEAPONRY

"...the tree swallow ...has even...made use of military hardware...at Fort Anne in old Annapolis Royal."

In the year 1945, in the month of June, the Moncton City Council received a postcard on which was written a message, short but very much to the point. It said:
City Council,
Moncton, N.B.
Dear Sirs:
May I bring your attention to the fact that, while pigeons are nice birds, they are also most annoying, as was the case when entering the Post Office today.
Sincerely,
Anon.

The City Council pondered this postcard and soon realized they had a touchy question on their hands. Nobody wants to be thought of as being opposed to birds, even pigeons, and certainly not a city councillor if he hopes to win the bird-watcher vote at the next election. Action on the pigeon issue was deferred until a later date and the matter quietly forgotten. But finally, in 1965, 20 years later, a more militant sector of the City Council, the Public Safety Committee, moved into the breach and with the judicious use of some chicken wire a solution was found to the hazards faced by Anonymous in getting in and out of the Moncton Post Office.

Now pigeons are well-known as disturbers of the peace, but only this past summer I discovered that the tree swallow has a pugnacious side to its nature, and has even been known to make use of military hardware, as it has been doing these past two years at Fort Anne in old Annapolis Royal. If you have been to Fort Anne you will remember that outside the museum, beside a path leading up to one of the entrance doors, stands a bronze cannon with a pyramid of cannon balls close by. I have been told that tree swallows have returned each year to this same cannon and are not to be frightened off by the nearness of the public. The swallows are determined to remain at their post, deep inside the cannon, and are ready to fly out heedlessly in the face of prying and curious tourists. Most of the Fort's 77,000 summer visitors pass within inches of the cannon's mouth and are directly in the line of flight.

When the swallows began building a nest inside the cannon, they attracted the camera buffs who tried to peer inside and get pictures of the fledgelings. Often they would end up with a black eye from one of the irate swallow parents. No one would dare to suggest that the swallows be removed from the cannon. They are almost as big a tourist attraction as the museum itself.

This just shows that there's nothing like a bird to get people all worked up and ready to come to its defence, as was the case in Pictou, N.S., when the double-crested cormorant faced a crisis.

The cormorant (in case you've never seen one) is a large ungainly sea bird, something like a stork. Colonies of them nest together in rookeries. In the spring of 1944 they established a rookery at Abercrombie Point, directly across the harbour from the town of Pictou and near the present Causeway. Tourists find them interesting and amusing. Thousands of motorists stop to photograph them. When these visitors get back home they tell their friends about them, and later on they too

"Colonies of cormorants nest together...across the harbour from...Pictou..."

come to visit Pictou. They stop in town and say they have heard about the cormorants and want to know where they can be seen. There are between 40 and 50 families of these unusual birds living here and according to the Pictou *Advocate* there is no other place on the 4,000 miles of Trans-Canada Highway where such a unique feature of wildlife can be observed within 50 feet of the road.

But recently there has been talk of installing street lighting along the Causeway, and some people in Pictou find the suggestion disturbing. They feel that electric lights pose a threat to the bird colony. As the Pictou *Advocate* says in a leading editorial, "The cormorants were brave enough to continue their nesting on the old pier pilings while heavy equipment was building the Causeway. But what effect would 24-hour lighting have? Would the parents continue nesting if they were denied the rest that is normal during the hours of darkness? It would," says the *Advocate*, "be a loss for Pictou

County and Nova Scotia if this living lesson in nature were driven away by man's zeal for 'progress.'"

And now, it seems, we have several species of birds flying in the very face of friendly relations with our neighbour to the South. They are in the thick of a border dispute between the U.S. and Canada, both of whom claim ownership of Machias Seal Island near the border between Maine and New Brunswick, one of the islands near Grand Manan. This lonely 15 acre ridge of granite out in the Bay of Fundy has been a matter of contention between the two countries for many years. Jack Russell, one of the three Canadian lighthouse keepers on Machias Seal Island, is more concerned about the birds that nest along its rocky shores. "It doesn't matter who owns the island," says Mr. Russell, "but it's a shame for the birds to become extinct just because there's not a bit of money to protect them."

Thousands of migratory birds stop here, most of them sea birds. It's the nesting place of the Puffins, the Arctic Terns, Razorbills, Leach's Storm-petrels, Savannah sparrows and a rare species of gull known as the Laughing Gull, from the sound of its call note.

During the nesting season Mr. Russell makes daily trips along the mile-long island to chase away gulls that swoop down on the eggs and nestlings of the smaller birds.

David Christie, curator of the New Brunswick Museum's natural science department in Saint John feels that the Canadian Wildlife Service should put a warden on the island. "If nothing is done," says Mr. Christie, "a new dispute over the ownership of the island will develop, this time not between nations but between bird species."

Sounds like all-out war. Should Mr. Christie's dire prediction come to pass we'd better call in the United Nations. Who knows? The birds just might decide that perhaps man was the enemy.

◆

Editor's Note: Happily the cormorants are still nesting in Pictou, but unhappily the Machias Seal Island dispute has not yet been settled.

THE POTENT POTATO

"…Maritimers have been a… potato-eating people."

At Hartland, New Brunswick, up the St. John River, in Carleton County, they hold a very special celebration—a festival to honour our most versatile vegetable, the potato. If potatoes are your favourite dish, Hartland is where you should go to feast on the season's new potatoes.

This is potato country. When you drive along the roads in Victoria County, it looks like one vast potato field and you understand why potatoes are the main vegetable eaten by Canadians—with New Brunswick and Prince Edward Island supplying 42 per cent of consumption. The headquarters of McCains Food Limited of Canada, the world's largest producer of frozen French fries, is at Florenceville, 19 km from Hartland.

From a long ways back, Maritimers have been a potato-growing and potato-eating people. Do you know how Nova Scotians came by that name Bluenose? It is because of a potato—a potato that used to be grown very widely in these parts, a blue potato that was called Bluenose. These potatoes were loaded aboard little coastal schooners and shipped down to Boston where the householders came to identify Nova Scotia with the Bluenose potato, so that finally they spoke of the people from Nova Scotia as Bluenoses. It was a bit of good-natured fun that Nova Scotians took to and soon they were proud to lay claim to being a Bluenose.

Not quite so gentle was the raillery in a potato folk song that originated in New Brunswick and was aimed at the inferior crops of potatoes grown in the State of Maine:

Oh potatoes they grown small over there
Oh potatoes they grown small over there
Oh potatoes they grown small
'Cause they plant them in the fall
And they eats them tops and all over there.

Which reminds us that potatoes are members of the deadly nightshade family. The tops or leaves of the plant are poisonous and could make you ill if you ate enough of them. That is exactly what happened when Sir Walter Raleigh returned from America with a bushel or two of spuds to introduce the new vegetable into Britain. Sir Walter's cook had, of course, never seen potatoes and had no idea how to prepare them, and, since the foliage had been brought back along with the tubers, he boiled the leaves and served *them* up instead of the potatoes, making Sir Walter very ill indeed. It so happened that Sir Walter was living in Ireland at the time, where he was governor, and his Irish cook finally learned how to cook potatoes and thought them delicious. He smuggled some out to his friends and neighbours and from then on a great love affair developed between the Irish and the potato. As one Irishman put it, "Be eating one potato, peeling a second, have a third in your fist and your eye on a fourth."

It is estimated that in the eighteenth and nineteenth centuries, Irishmen ate an average of ten pounds of potatoes a day. During this time, a dramatic improvement in health took place and the population increased rapidly.

The English, however, did not take advantage of the miraculous new vegetable. Common folk turned their noses up at them, maintaining that there could be little good in a plant ignored by scripture...and eaten by Irishmen.

This ignorant prejudice still persists in the widespread myth that potatoes are fattening. If you are a calorie-counter, consider this. Suppose you ate a lunch consisting of a doughnut, a glass of malted milk, and a serving of strawberry shortcake, and then ate exactly the same number of calories in the form of potatoes. How many potatoes would you have to eat? Three? Six? Ten? You would, in fact, have to consume twelve—an even dozen good-sized potatoes—to equal the same number of calories as you would get in that relatively modest lunch.

Before calorie-counting became fashionable, the people of Lunenburg knew intuitively that potatoes were good for them. One of their traditional dishes is a sort of potato chowder called *Kartoffelsuppe*.

The Acadians, too, developed their own specialty—or *Pâté à la Rapure*—Rappie Pie made from grated potatoes.

Potatoes have been used not only as a food, but as a medicine as well. There are those who claim that a slice of raw potato is good for a burn. Others carry a potato in their pocket to prevent rheumatism. It is even employed in the care of the skin. The famous French herbalist, Maurice Messegue, recommends a mask of chopped potatoes, claiming that it moisturizes the skin and banishes wrinkles.

No other vegetable provides so much health and energy as the potato. It is our good fortune to live in the very heart of Canada's principal potato-growing region.

So don't forget the Potato Festival at Hartland, new Brunswick, where you can sample all sorts of potato dishes—baked, boiled, or crisp French-fries.

❖

Editor's Note: The Hartland Potato Festival has been held in early July for more than 30 years.

THE GAMES CHILDREN PLAY

A neighbour of mine has been having problems with his son. It seems the boy next door has one of these skateboards and the two boys have been trying it out. My neighbour isn't happy about this. He took his son aside and said, "Look, I don't want you playing with that skateboard any more."

"Why not?" the boy asked.

"Because you'll end up breaking it and then his parents will expect *me* to buy a new one. And I can't afford to fork out forty dollars!"

"Forty dollars!" I said.

"Yes—these things are expensive."

Well, I looked in the mail order catalogue and there they were—skateboards, all the way from $17 to $39.98. But that is only a part of it! You have to buy elbow pads (so if the rider upsets he will not shatter his elbows), and knee pads (to keep him from breaking his legs) and a helmet (so he won't fracture his skull). By the time you get a skateboarder properly outfitted, it's the best part of $70.

While I was glancing through the catalogue, I noticed the prices of some other items intended for the amusement and gaiety of children...such as training suits for jogging ($19.98) and jogging shoes (which I used to call sneakers). They are now selling for $29.98

and up. Of course you have all kinds of hockey gear to protect arms, legs, ankles, shins, shoulders, and teeth...along with a pair of goalie pads (they're selling for $99.98).

It used to be, not too long ago, that the kids in my neighbourhood did their skating on Sade's Pond and played hockey with a crooked alder bush, but that's not fun any more. You have to have the gear. First, of course, you have to have the money to *buy* the gear.

I see here they're even selling a pair of stilts. That is something we all made for ourselves when I was growing up...out of a pair of discarded clothes-line poles. Now they're selling for $10 a pair.

Children are being denied the fun of doing these things for themselves. They are being robbed of something else, too.

Only 20 years ago, children here in the Maritimes possessed a rich folklore of games which required no gear whatever, or only such gear as could be extemporized on the spur of the moment. Adults had nothing whatever to do with this. It was a child culture—one generation of children passing this treasure-house of games along to the next, along with the appropriate jingles and directions.

There was "Here We Go Round the

Mulberry Bush" and "The Farmer in the Dell."
Another one started out, "I'm an old man
from Botany Bay...what have you got to give
me today?" There was "Ring Around a Rosey,"
and "Take a Giant Step," and "London Bridge
is Falling Down."

None of these is being played in our school-
yards today. Hopscotch is still hanging on.
They still play tag and do some skipping, but
the little ones do most of their playing among
the mechanical playground equipment we've
supplied them with—the slides and teeter-
totters and monkey bars.

They're not even playing marbles any more.
I asked for some at our local hardware store
but they don't carry them now. The familiar
net bags of red and green and orange marbles
are now a thing of the past.

Let's, for a moment, look back to a time
before TV and the mail order catalogue took
over and see how the children managed to
amuse themselves.

In Stellarton, N.S., they played a game
called Peggy. All you needed was a three-foot
length from an old broom handle and a six-
inch length from the same handle for a
"peggy." The object was to hit the peggy with
the broom handle as far as you could without
the opposing player catching it.

Other games popular in Stellarton were
"King and the Golden Rod," "Bull-in-the-
Ring" and "Hoist Your Sail." This was a terrific
game. You had several players taking sides.

*"Only 20 years ago, children...possessed a rich folk-
lore of games which required no gear whatever..."*

Hantsport School, 1943.

One group would run off and hide in the bushes and the leader of the other side had to try to find them. When he got too close to them, the captain of the other team would shout, "Hoist your sails!" and everyone would run like mad for home base.

There was a tremendous lot of running in these games. There was "Run, Sheep, Run," once a well-known game around Dartmouth. In parts of New Brunswick they had a chasing game known as "Hares and Hounds," where one or two boys or girls were given a head start and then the other team tried to catch them. (In Prince Edward Island the same game was known as "Fox and Hound.") Just simple running was excitement enough for most kids.

The other day I came on a marvellous account of a little red school house in New Brunswick, a school that had once served the community of Salmon Creek, several miles above Grand Lake, in Queens County. Here is how the writer describes a game once played at Salmon Creek. He says,

While it can hardly be called a game, one of our amusements in the months when there was no snow on the ground was 'running home'. If someone was feeling particularly full of energy as the group left the school at four o'clock, he might say 'Let's run home.' If the others were in an equally energetic mood they would say, 'Let's!' So away we would go, not running fast or racing each other, but on the other hand never stopping to walk.

In most of these games, nobody bothered keeping score or worrying over who won. It was the *game* that was important. Up to about 20 years ago, there was a popular game in my neighbourhood called "Harley Over." To play this all you needed was a ball and a building of some kind—a house or a barn, preferably with a high roof. The players stood on opposite sides of the building, so they couldn't see each other. Then one of them would shout, "Harley over!"— and hurl the ball up over the roof. His partner was supposed to catch it...but nobody was there to see whether he *did* catch it, so it really didn't matter. The important thing was to shout "Harley over!" and throw the ball up over the roof. Sometimes they'd keep at this for the best part of an hour. It is one of the games children no longer play.

I've not even mentioned "Mumbly Peg," or "Duck on a Rock," or "Jack Stones," or "Go Through the Broom Handle." All of them were part of a magical, safe, energetic, and friendly folklore which our children once kept green and that is now almost extinct. Why?

It didn't cost anything. There was no gear to buy.

◆

Editor's note: Prices quoted as of 1978, 20 years ago.

HOW TO KEEP MOSQUITOES AT BAY

"...whether you use Muskol, orange peelings, face nets, or take a stiff slug of...rum..."

At this season, many vacationists are leaving the city's rush and clamour for a few weeks of quiet country living. I hope they find it.

The city isn't the only place where your nerves can be frazzled. The country has its quota of spiteful irritations and among them is a tiny creature that can turn the pleasantest summer afternoon into a misery of bites, swots, and buzzing persistence.

The mosquito is still with us, and this summer they're worse than ever. An exceptionally cool, damp spring is made to order for the breeding and raising of healthy mosquitoes with hearty appetites.

You'd think, by now, the entomologists would have ammunition enough to eliminate this nuisance but, except for eradication campaigns close to some of our cities, the mosquito is doing business at the old stand and is able to create panic in those who are allergic to the bite.

To get an idea of just how bad it can be, here's how one early visitor to Nova Scotia felt about the mosquitoes. Luke Harrison, writing home from Nova Scotia to his brother in England, in the year 1774, puts it this way: *We do not like the country, nor never shall. The mosquitoes are a terrible plague in this country. You may think that mosquitoes cannot hurt, but if you do you are mistaken, for they will swell your legs and hands so that some persons are blind and lame for days. They grow worse every year...and they bite the English the worst.*

Well, I can assure you they're still biting. So how can we avoid them? What can we do to keep them away?

There are many theories. Some say the best method is to drink plenty of booze. Others suggest eating garlic or onions. But the experts claim that nothing you can eat will repel a biting insect once he's on the warpath.

One thing the scientists do know for sure. If you wear dark clothing, you are asking for trouble. That, more than anything else, seems to attract the mosquito—especially blue denim. Blue denim is so bad that the experts use it to bait their fly traps.

Mosquitoes love warmth and humidity, along with a little grit, so it is best to keep cool and bathe often.

It seems they favour adults rather than children, men rather than women. Perhaps this is because all the biting is done by the female mosquito, the male remaining strictly vegetarian in his diet.

Some have held that we bring these attacks upon ourselves as retribution for unrighteous behaviour. In fact, we have an early manuscript that rather proves this point. The summer of 1795 was a bad one for mosquitoes around the Tantramar marshes. Along the isthmus of Chignecto, people were being almost eaten up alive. So some of them got together and called on a Jesuit friar to come and do something about it. Well, he could hardly refuse. He did at length come and, as the manuscript explains,

...having all the things prepared, he took a basin of holy water, a staff with a little brush, and having on his white robe, went about the marshes with about thirty following in the procession. A young lad, going before him, bearing the holy water, sprinkled the marshes on each side of him, a little bell jingling at the same time, and all singing the words ora pro nobis. They wheeled about and turned.... Thus they passed and repassed across the Tantramar marshes, the mosquitoes all the while rising before them, only to light behind them. Finally, the friar announced that it was impossible to prevail over the

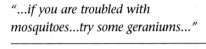

"...if you are troubled with mosquitoes...try some geraniums..."

mosquitoes...so great were the sins of the people of Chignecto.

By the way, if you are troubled with mosquitoes and flies getting into your house or apartment, try some geraniums in the window box. Or calceolarias. The scent of geraniums and calceolarias is offensive to flies and mosquitoes, and thus, acts as a barrier to these pests.

They are also kept off by the smell of orange or lemon peel, which gives you a chance to recycle those orange peelings by rubbing them on your hands and face.

Of course, there are a number of commercial insect repellents on the market—some in pressurized spray cans, some packed as creams or liquids in plastic squeeze bottles. Among them is one called Muskol, brainchild of Colonel Charlie Coll, a native of Pictou County. Muskol was originally manufactured right here in the Maritimes at Hilden, near Truro.

So whether you use Muskol, orange peelings, face nets, or take a stiff slug of Jamaica rum, remember, when you start out on your vacation, that like every other year, this one promises to be a vintage year for mosquitoes.

◆

GOVERNOR MURRAY AND THE ROSE BUSHES

"...we have these power lawn-mowers to make the work... so easy." Norm photographed at a neighbour's.

A legal battle without precedent is being fought in the courts of Pennsylvania. The editor of a gardening magazine, Robert Rodale, is testing the individual's right to not mow his front lawn—or at least not in the conventional manner. What he's testing really, is just how inclined we all are to submit to the example of our neighbours by manicuring the front lawn each Saturday morning so that it looks exactly like every other property along the street.

In itself, this is hardly a world-shaking issue, especially when we have these power lawn-mowers and riding lawn-mowers to make the work of mowing the lawn so easy. So, why not go along with the rest of the street?

But the fact that it's being tested in the courts, suggests that some people are ready to resist public pressure and try something new in the way of a lawn—perhaps some sort of ground cover, like ground ivy or periwinkle, rather than Kentucky bluegrass.

It is strange how we've allowed ourselves to develop this grass-cutting ritual to the point where nobody wants to step out of line. Are we so desperately afraid of what people might say? Or is it simply that we don't want to upset the neighbours by seeming to challenge the way *they* do things?

Of course when it comes to our deep-down convictions, it is impossible to go along with all the neighbours, some of whom don't vote the way do, or don't go to the same church. Yet, nobody holds that against us. It is only this business of mowing the lawn. Then...we all think alike, unwilling to differ on something so conspicuous as a front lawn.

It is a good thing we don't have Governor John Murray living in the neighbourhood because this early governor of Cape Breton Island didn't give two hoots for public opinion.

Governor Murray was not the kind to curry favour with anyone. Even before his appointment as governor of Cape Breton, he had a run-in with his rival in Halifax, John Despard, who was also seeking the Cape Breton assignment. Despard was no match for John Murray when it came to expressing strong opinions. On days when Murray had had a twinge or two of gout, he could muster a flaming sense of indignation that swept all argument to the winds.

Irascible, hot-tempered John Murray did not conceal his contempt for the foppish schemers in Halifax who fluttered about Governor Wentworth. But they enjoyed a telling advantage because they were there, close to the seat of government, while Murray was in Cape Breton.

John Despard finally gained the ear of Governor Wentworth. He dropped hints that Cape Breton's new governor, away off there down in Sydney, was grossly abusing his office, building a mansion for himself with public monies, surrounded by sweeping lawns, winding paths, and lavish plantings of rose bushes, and beds of tulips.

There was a certain amount of truth in all this. Governor Murray *was* building up a beautiful flower garden; much of the work he'd done himself. But as to the governor's mansion, there was nothing very ambitious about the house he lived in. It was rather modest, in fact. John Murray's interest lay in his garden, not in stately hallways and fine furniture. He was always sending down to Boston for packets of flower seeds. (This would be around about 1800.) He imported unusual plants and shrubs from Scotland and would be up early in the morning, before sunrise, to see what new roses might be in bloom.

One Sunday morning, while the people of Sydney were in church, a ship sailed up the harbour and cast anchor near the barracks and a long-boat rowed ashore. At the close of the service, as the Governor emerged from church, he was met at the door by an orderly who thrust a letter into his hand—a letter informing him that he had been replaced...by his rival, John Despard. The new governor, even at this very moment, waited out on his ship in the harbour for Governor Murray to hand over the keys and other insignia of authority. In short, Governor Murray was to vacate his official residence right away...today.

John Murray was furious. To be dismissed so curtly, at such short notice...and forced to relinquish his damask roses, his daylilies and sweet-smelling wallflowers, to a man he despised.

Well, he could have the governorship—but not before John Murray had had his say. He'd show them in Halifax how he felt.... Not in words, this message would be written in letters of fire.

He ordered his servants to search the barn for straw and litter and to pile all this straw on top of the flowers and rose bushes, along with baskets of chips and kindlings. Then he carried, from the kitchen, a burning ember and tossed it among the straw.

Soon the fragrance of his roses gave way to the acrid smell of smoke. The beautiful flower garden burst into flames that could be seen across the harbour. Within half an hour, the garden, into which he had poured so much of his frustration...and love, was finally reduced to a desolation of bare earth and scorched roots.

When word of what he had done spread throughout Sydney, his friends were stunned at the news. But many of them respected John Murray in spite of his hot-tempered ways, even because of them. He was a very human man, John Murray. Those among his neighbours who shared his fondness for flowers felt they understood why he had put his garden to the torch. They would even have forgiven him if he had chosen *not* to mow his front lawn.

*"Governor Murray...would be up...before sunrise,
to see what new roses might be in bloom."*

LUMBAGO—AND
TOSSING THE CABER

The other day I went out to the garden to get some potatoes and as I began digging, suddenly, I found myself unable to straighten up. If you've never had lumbago, I sincerely hope you never do. It can be embarrassingly unpredictable. It makes you think twice before leaning over to pick up the newspaper, or even tie your shoelaces.

It gives you a new respect for those who go in for weight-lifting and throwing the discus or tossing the caber—as they do at the Festival of the Tartans, at Trenton and New Glasgow, and also at the Gaelic Mod at St. Annes, Cape Breton. No sign of lumbago there.

In these highland games, you can't afford to have back trouble. Your back must be in absolutely A-1 shape, able to take any strain you subject it to. And the feats of strength these Scotsmen perform are impressive.

Not only the Scots, the Irish, too, have produced some powerful physiques. One of the strongest men who ever lived in Nova Scotia was an Irishman, John Orpin, who spent his life in the little coastal port of Morden, on the Fundy shore.

Once, while over in Saint John, N.B., he was challenged to enter a weight-lifting contest by some crewmen from a ship tied up at the wharf. They'd heard about this Samson from Nova Scotia...but could he lift a 400-pound anchor? Orpin could quite honourably have declined the challenge. After all, at the time, in 1858, he was 54 years old and the two who wanted to test him were young men in their prime. However, he gladly offered to take on the anchor. First, the second mate stepped forward and lifted the anchor two inches into the air before he let it fall. Then one of the deckhands, a giant Swede, weighing 250 pounds, raised it some two feet off the deck. Now it was John Orpin's turn. He lifted the anchor, then holding it with the shank upright, he told his challengers to stand one on each side of the flukes. With the added human cargo, he lifted the anchor off the deck. From then on, no one questioned his right to be known as the Samson of the Annapolis Valley.

Stories about men like John Orpin suggest such abounding good health that you wonder where it all came from. What gave these men such fantastic strength? Most of them were of quite normal height. They were not giants, like Cape Breton's Angus MacAskill. There is no suggestion that they went in for any special training, like getting ready for the Pan-Am Games, or the Olympics. They were simply strong to begin with.

There *was* a certain amount of local rivalry—at Gairloch, for instance, in Pictou County, where for many years men vied with each other in trying to lift a certain big stone on the side of the road, near the property known as the Alex Sutherland place. One man, Big Murdoch MacKenzie, could let air under it. The local school master, William Ross, could lift it one inch off the ground. Alex Sutherland, or 'little' Alex Sutherland, as they called him, could lift it up to his knees! It became known as the 'lifting stone' of Gairloch. In 1923, it was taken to Pictou town to the *Hector* Celebration and that is where it is today. Although hundreds have tried to lift it since then, only one man, a man by the name of Grant from Caribou, was able to raise it off the ground.

It was men such as these, with their strong backs, who carved out from the wilderness the stump-land farms of our ancestors. Some claim that much of their strength could be attributed to a diet of Scotch barley broth, oatmeal porridge, and bannock bread.

Whatever the reason, the brawn of these early Highlanders was amazing. In Pictou and Antigonish, you still hear stories of men who carried immense burdens on their backs, such as a grindstone weighing 300 pounds, because there were no roads through the forest—not even bridle paths. You either carried these supplies yourself, or you went without.

In Antigonish County, after the crops began to grow, they found themselves with wheat but no mill at which to have it ground. So they put the wheat in sacks and carried it miles through the forest to a grist mill in Guysborough. Then they lugged the flour all the way back home.

Those of us with back troubles, can only stand (if we *can* stand) in awe, at the stories about such men as Lauchy Mor McIsaac of Arisaig who on a spring day, through slush and snow, up three miles of steep mountain, carried a barrel of mackerel from John McEachern's in Dunmaglass, to his own shanty on top of the mountain.

Donald McNeil of Morristown, while engaged in building a vessel, sent four men to fetch an anchor weighing 650 pounds, that had been landed on the beach some distance away. When they failed in the job, he himself went and carried it back in his arms. No lumbago there.

Doctors report that, today, one out of every three adults suffers some form of back pain. With the exception of respiratory diseases, back pain causes more people to visit doctors' offices than any other medical complaint.

Why do we today get this ailment? Doctors persist in a never-ending battle over the basic cause of low back pain. Some say it is the result of faulty habits of posture, with too much sitting and not enough standing and walking. Others look to the stomach muscles and prescribe special exercises as a vital part of bad-back therapy. Overweight patients are invariably advised to slim down. Others, specifically psychiatrists, believe a great deal of chronic back trouble is psychosomatic in origin. Treatments themselves are just as varied in nature as the suspected causes, ranging from simple aspirin to surgery. If only we had someone like Donald McNeil or Lauchy Mor McIsaac to give us a few pointers on how to keep the back functioning without complaint.

Luckily, their descendants are still able to show us how to toss the caber, and you can see them doing just that at the Festival of the Tartans in New Glasgow and at the Gaelic Mod in St. Annes, or at other Cape Breton Festivals and Games which take place in July and August every year. ◆

"...Luckily their descendants show us how to toss the caber..."

A SUMMER TO REMEMBER

There's been some talk lately about the need to re-examine our school textbooks to make sure they are properly Canadian—especially our history books. It is felt that we have not presented ourselves in a sufficiently flattering light, and I agree. We've been far too modest. We've underplayed some of our finest achievements, and among these is a war, little noted in our textbooks and remembered only locally, in the provinces of New Brunswick and Nova Scotia, called the Fenian Raid.

It took place in the year 1866, on the border between Canada and the United States and its most exciting episodes occurred near the seaside town of St. Andrews, New Brunswick, at the mouth of the St. Croix River. On one side of the river is Canada; on the other side is the United States.

The Fenians were a group of Irish immigrants in the United States, who nurtured the traditional Irish hatred of England. They cherished a dream that the territory north of the border might be freed from the British yoke, with the connivance, or even assistance, of the American authorities.

Fortunately for Canada, most Americans were not impressed. The Fenians went ahead with their plans nonetheless.

Blockhouse built in 1812.
"...near the sea-side town of St. Andrews, N.B."

On April 10, 1866, the first group of Fenians arrived in Eastport, along the coast from St. Andrews, on the American side of the border. They had a schooner loaded with arms and munitions. Soon, Fenian troops could be seen drilling on the fields near Robbinston, across the river from St. Andrews.

The authorities on the Canadian side sprang to action. A call went out for volunteers to defend the border. The militia was called up in Saint John. Regular troops from Halifax were rushed to St. Andrews. Everywhere throughout the Maritimes, men were volunteering to go to fight the Fenians. Women were tearfully saying goodbye to their husbands as bands marched down to the station to see them off. The fever of war was in the air.

In Halifax, an enterprising merchant on Granville Street had this advertisement in the paper: "Just received...cases containing revolvers...the very articles for popping off Fenians."

Across the province, volunteers were drilling at Chester, Bridgewater, Liverpool, Shelburne, Barrington, Yarmouth, Weymouth, Digby, Annapolis, and Windsor. People waited for the alarm to be sounded by the ringing of church bells and toots on factory whistles. Bonfires along the shore would send their message into the night if enemy craft should appear.

Along St. Marys Bay, in Digby County, a rumour got started that American ships were about to raid Sissibou. The militia was quickly summoned and that night they stationed a guard at Shook's Point. During the night the sentries heard a crackling in the bushes. Without a moment's hesitation, they fired their muskets in the direction of the noise... and discovered that they had killed Deacon Shook's cow.

Meanwhile, around St. Andrews itself, those not in the militia formed themselves into a Home Guard. They drilled every day. Their uniform, which each man provided for himself, consisted principally of a flannel coat of eye-catching red.

During the months that followed, St. Andrews became a perfect hive of activity. The streets bristled with soldiers. Some of the ladies reminisced years later that it was the gayest summer the town had ever known, with handsome young officers in scarlet tunics, ships of war patrolling the St. Croix River, and about it all a delightful element of danger. As one of them recalled, "just enough to be interesting—without being alarming." There were many parties and private theatricals.... It was a summer to remember.

Well, the Fenians never did come across the border. It was not that they lacked courage. I think it was simply that they did not have the heart to disturb the people of St. Andrews, who were having such a wonderful time. Whatever the reason, they finally decided to stop marching back and forth on the fields across the water from St. Andrews. They disbanded and went back home to Boston and New York. And that was the Fenian Raid.

If only our wars today could be conducted in such a civilized manner! In those days, the people of New Brunswick had mastered the secret of how to carry on a war without anyone getting hurt, and with everyone—except Deacon Shook's cow—having a good time.

There is a happy little footnote to the Fenian Raid. Fifty years later, in 1912, the Canadian Government recognized there was something unique about this war. They marked the event by issuing to a few surviving veterans a special medal and a cheque for one hundred dollars.

◆

THE GREAT SPRINGHILL-PARRSBORO BASEBALL GAME

When it comes to baseball, it is pretty hard to beat the World Series for excitement. Hard—but not impossible. It has been done. The most exciting baseball game I ever heard tell of was not included in the World Series. It took place in the town of Parrsboro in the year 1939, a game between the hometown team and the Springhill Red Sox. Before I describe the game itself, I should give you a little background on this.

For many years, the Nova Scotia towns of Springhill and Parrsboro shared a common interest in the coal industry. Springhill had the mines—and the miners—but it was inland, some 20 miles from the nearest port. Much of the coal mined in Springhill was transported from Springhill to Parrsboro on a railroad built by the Cumberland Railway and Coal Company, and, here in the bustling little port of Parrsboro, it was loaded onto vessels.

The two towns were held together by this common interest in coal. It was for many years a very profitable relationship, and a very happy one. In fact, the miners of Springhill always came over to Parrsboro for their annual picnic, which was held sometime during the last week in July or the first week in August. At this time the mines in Springhill would be closed down for repairs and the miners would then go on their annual vacation. Then would take place what was known as the Miners' Picnic.

Special cars were borrowed from the Canadian National Railway. Some 5,000

...the Parrsboro team challenged Springhill to a game at the Miners' Picnic."

people, miners and their families and friends, would make the train journey over to Parrsboro for this tremendous outing, a sort of miners' festival. Every year the kids and grown-ups looked forward to it. The people in Parrsboro looked forward to welcoming their friends and the people in Springhill looked forward to the outing and enjoying the hospitality of the people of Parrsboro. It was a grand affair, the day of the Miners' Picnic.

Occasionally, however, these picnics were marred—or perhaps one should say enlivened—by entertainments that were not on the official programme.

Now some of this is merely hearsay. I have not been able to verify every point. I am just telling it to you as it was told to me by some old timers along the Parrsboro shore.

The first of these little irregularities took place at one of these Miners' Picnics back around about 1900. For some reason there was a difference of opinion between a man from Springhill and a man from Parrsboro. Liquor may have had something to do with it. At any rate it built up into a violent argument which turned into a fist fight. Others joined in. The momentum of the thing gathered force. The miners from Springhill came rushing forward to defend their position, the Parrsboro men were soon calling in reinforcements, and perhaps because the Parrsboro men were fighting on their own soil, they were able to drive the Springhill men back to the special train, into which they retreated. Rocks were hurled. The

railway cars were attacked, every window in the cars was smashed, until finally the locomotive was forced into putting on steam and heading back to Springhill.

As I say, I am not sure when this famous battle took place. It must have been around the turn of the century, or perhaps even before that time. It left surprisingly little rancour. It certainly did not prevent the miners from returning to Parrsboro next summer for their annual picnic. In fact, this event continued, year after year, until the final picnic was held in the summer of 1939.

In the previous year, the Maritime Junior Baseball Championship had been won by the Springhill Red Sox. So the Parrsboro team challenged Springhill to a game at the Miners' Picnic.

As usual it was a gala day. Thousands came over to Parrsboro on the special trains from Springhill. The game was held in the ballpark up on the school grounds. Everything seemed to be going along peacefully enough until Parrsboro started drawing ahead. By the seventh inning they were obviously on a winning streak, with a lead of four runs, and at this point something happened. Out in the bleachers an altercation began between two men—a man from Springhill and a man from Parrsboro—and again it developed into a fight.

To understand why this took place—because I don't think it would take place today—we must remind ourselves of something most of us have forgotten all about or know of only

"The fight moved...slowly...onto Main Street."

vaguely, from what our parents have told us. Those grim years were known as The Depression or the Hungry Thirties. During these belt-tightening years very few were able to afford imported Scotch whiskey, or even Jamaica rum. They had to rely on their native ingenuity, and certain home-made beverages enjoyed a wide popularity, such as malt beer, hard cider, bee beer. One of these drinks, known locally as Parrsboro Champagne, was a combination of orange pop and various household ingredients.

Perhaps it was these home-made refreshments, or possibly the memory of that other fight so many years ago.... It all started very naturally. The Parrsboro man was elated that his team was winning. There were the usual jibes and taunts. Then some of the Springhill men in the bleachers felt that it was up to them to give tangible evidence of their support for the home team and somehow it got going.

This fight had a Homeric quality about it. As it developed, it grew bigger and spread. It augmented itself with little pockets of shouting men who rose up from the bleachers, arguing hotly, until finally the game stopped and pretty much everyone in the ball park became involved either as an onlooker or a participant. The fight moved, like a great cluster of swarming bees, slowly down over school hill, onto Main Street.

The Mounted Police were there, and the railway police. They could do nothing; they were powerless. The battle continued on for almost two hours and ended in a draw— largely due to exhaustion.

I never did learn what the final score of that game was. Apparently it never got any further than the seventh inning.

Now, as we settle back to another World Series, and catch the faint, feeble cries of "Kill the Umpire!" we think back to that wonderful ball game of 1939, when the Springhill Red Sox held out against Parrsboro until the seventh inning.

◆

THE WINDS OF AUGUST

I believe it was a Canadian who coined the phrase "good grey Canadian," to let his neighbour know just how unimaginative and torpid a fellow he is. There is some truth in it. Enthusiasm comes hard to us; we don't go for things all out. There always seems to be somebody holding back.

Today, for example, I received a copy of the new edition of the mail order catalogue, the Fall and Winter Edition. Here it is August, the water at the beach is just warming up nicely—and now this has to come.

"A wind has come up, sweeping across the river..."

I refuse to be disheartened. August has been too long getting here. I am going to enjoy every last golden moment of it, and no one shall bluff me into contemplating the delights of nylon ski jackets and fleece-lined underwear.

But then nothing could cast a shadow on days such as these. How wonderful to waken in the morning and find that you've slept with only one blanket. After breakfast, you feel too confined in the house and wander about the garden, to watch the hummingbirds darting among the Chinese forget-me-nots. The leaves on the big maple glisten under a fleckless sky and are still hanging there attentive to the morning sounds. Your senses seem sharpened to an unaccustomed awareness. You wonder what is going to happen, for something special must surely happen on such a day as this.

A wind has come up, sweeping across the river; the waves glint and come scurrying ashore to chatter against the beach. It is a hot wind, filled with the memory of Johnny Pye weed, and golden rod, and bulrushes where the cows come down to drink.

Tonight there will be a long warm evening, with car lights moving out onto the government wharf, where one may park and listen to the tide lapping in. A dance is on at the Community Centre. One could go swimming at midnight. There are so many glorious things to do on such a night.

The August winds are talking to us, telling us of a thousand adventures if only we could reach out and pluck some excitement from them before they sweep on and away from us—like life itself.

In the winter, there will be time enough to withdraw and brood beside our dull Canadian firesides. We have been handed these precious, numbered days of August, filled with the promise of untold joys. It is there in the wind, waiting for us. What is stopping us? Why don't we strike out now, answer the wind's call and follow where it leads?

Yes, it is an incredible month, this month of August; a frightening month, too. For this is the month when the wars begin. The Franco-Prussian war began on August 4 in 1870. On another August 4, the World War of 1914 started. The Second World War, too, germinated and exploded under this hot midsummer sun. It is a dangerous month, August.

Why do you suppose those wars began in August? Do you suppose someone felt (as I did) that today something should happen? Did he feel he had lingered too long, that life's

"We have been handed these precious, numbered days of August..."
Norm and his niece by the Avon River.

elusive essence waited for him across the next border? Was it time to go out and follow the wind?

I wonder if it is such an admirable trait, this taking action, this getting so excited about things? Perhaps, in our good grey Canadian way, the Fall and Winter mail order catalogue isn't such a bad idea.... I see that my neighbour next door has *his* copy. He is lying there in the back yard on his *chaise longe*, sipping iced tea, leafing through those 600 glossy pages, and dreaming of snow tires and sheepskin lined overshoes. He is not going to cross any border this August, and I don't think I will either.

◆

autumn

SEPTEMBER
OUR SECRET TREASURE

"...you have to wait until September for the fattest ears of corn."
Norm in his garden.

So it's all over—the whole gorgeous, impossible, unsettling business we call vacation time has come to an end. At the seaside, they are swimming out to the life-raft for the last time. On the beach they are gathering up blankets, towels, transistors and binoculars. The beach umbrellas are coming down, people are saying good-bye, exchanging names and addresses, promising to write, and clustering in smiling groups to project onto that last roll of film the brave insouciance of one who has just completed three weeks holiday with pay.

Here at home, we've helped pack the tent into the back of the station wagon, strapped the baby's play-pen on top of the luggage, asked to be remembered to Aunt Bertha, hoped they'd have a good crossing on the ferry. Then there are more good-byes as the car backs out onto the road, blows its farewell tattoo...and they've gone.

Back in the kitchen, there is still coffee simmering on the stove, so let's pour ourselves a cup and sit here for a moment to contemplate how we and our friends and relatives—from Columbus, Ohio, or Thunder Bay, Ontario—have been having a wonderful time.

This matter of vacations is of peculiar interest to us here in the Maritimes because for the most of us this is the one time of year we *have* vacations—those two shining months of July and August. In places like Florida, vacation time goes on all year round, endlessly, one long sunny day after another. Here, it is all crowded into these few precious weeks when the thermometer allows us to wear shorts and a V-neck sweat shirt and sit out on the verandah after sundown. It is further compressed as we pass Labour Day and the school buses begin to run. As someone said to me the other day, "Who wants to be on vacation in September when the kids are back in school? You like to enjoy your vacation with your family." So, for most of us, vacation time is July and August.

It is then that we are offered this tantalizing revelation of what life might be—a frustrating glimpse of all the fun we've been missing; of how good it is to relax in the sunshine and feel grass under our bare feet. We are handed these two or three disturbing weeks, and then, just as we're beginning to savour the delights of sleeping in in the morning, it is all snatched away from us and we must scurry back to the job, in Boston, or Toronto.

It sweeps upon us, this vacation phenomenon, like a great wave of trailer camps and suntan lotion and blueberries to be picked. Here come the cousins from New Hampshire and Winnipeg who haven't been home in thirty years. Of course there's a round of coffee parties and outings so everybody can meet them and assure each other...they haven't changed one bit.

It would be a truly wonderful time, if only there *was* the time. But of course there isn't. The vacation runs its panting course for two or three weeks and then suddenly the school bell rings, the curtain is rung down on all this frenzied relaxation, and we are left here all alone, with the quiet of September upon us and rolls of undeveloped film, thinking back to all the things we might have done, but didn't.

It is like handing a child a ticket to Disneyland and saying, "Here, go ahead, enjoy yourself. You can take in anything you like, the magic castle, the marching bands, Mickey Mouse, whatever you like...only, we'll be leaving in five minutes. Go ahead, enjoy yourself, it's all there, the whole thing, it's all yours." That is what summertime is like for most of us—just too wonderful to cope with.

And so, perhaps as a sort of bonus, nature has designed the quieter, more reasonable month of September. Summer visitors never see us at our best in this month that lies ahead. The sweltering heatwave is over. We settle down to cool nights and clear days—days that challenge us to ignore the pink petunias in the window planter, and to keep from gazing at our neighbour's border of snapdragons and golden calendula. This is the month to visit the Public Gardens in Halifax or take a stroll through the Pioneer Flower Garden at Kings Landing, 23 miles west of Fredericton, N.B., on the Trans-Canada Highway.

So few of our guests stay on into September

sunshine. They miss so much by going back home when the school bell rings. It is only now that the tomatoes are really ripe...and you have to wait into September for the fattest ears of corn.

Think of driving all the way down from Ontario, and just as the Gravenstein apples are ready to make into a deep-apple pie, turning around and having to leave. If they would stay just one week longer...but few of them ever do. So we are left sadly holding the deep-apple pie and having to eat it all by ourselves.

But you know, I think many of these things, like vacations, summertime and so on, are really experienced more richly in retrospect, or in anticipation, than in reality. So let us look forward to what's in store for us. All those rolls of undeveloped film are snapshots to be exchanged at Christmas, together with memories of what a wonderful summer it was. Then we can start to make plans for all the exciting things we're going to do...next summer.

◆

"...the Gravenstein apples are ready..."

Our Fall Fairs and Exhibitions

If you happen to be a farmer, living in Prince Edward Island, then you are classified by the federal government as being in Canada's lowest income group.

It's true. Says so here in a volume called "Taxation Statistics," issued by the Department of National Revenue. Your income, the income of a farmer, is among the lowest in all Canada.

So I'm going to pose you a question. In view of the fact that you could earn a better income doing almost anything else, why in the world do people continue to go farming in P.E.I.—or anywhere else in the Maritimes, for that matter? What strange fascination holds people to such a poverty-stricken occupation?

To explore this secret, now that the plums and cucumbers and curly-leaf cabbage are ripening on the vine and the air is heady with the smell of mustard pickles, let's go to the County Fair. Here, surrounded by the fragrance of prize-winning African violets and sweet peas, or out in the raucous blare of the midway, let's see if we can't find something in the way of an answer.

The first impression of the County Fair is of people, like myself, who have come here simply to take in the show, to stand gaping at things—like the ox-pulling contest—while consuming prodigious quantities of French fries with ketchup.

The crowd drifts idly about, sampling franks and hamburgers, cotton candy and caramel corn, listening to the pitchmen, and perhaps taking a turn on the Ferris wheel, as if they were here merely to be amused.

Then you notice something. This young man who was trying on a western hat at one of the booths on the midway, you meet five minutes later in the shed housing the beef cattle...only now he's at work with a curry-comb, shining up the glossy coat of a Hereford heifer. You discover he is a member of the 4-H club, with several red and blue ribbons tacked up on the hitching post. And the pigtailed girl he was with...she's leading her pony out to the show ring. Then you begin to get the feeling that all these idle spectators, in some way know each other, that they're part of a family—the farming community.

As you continue on through the sheep shed you come on two old men who have stopped to renew acquaintance.

*Pumpkins,
Windsor, N.S.*

"Yes, I was workin' in the Cumberland lumber woods that winter...Teamster...We got up at two thirty every morning...Started work at four. Worked in the woods by lantern light. All ax work them days, no saws....Yes, times have changed...."

You look about at the crowd now with more attention. They are not here as strangers; they are here, some of them, for perhaps their fiftieth season. Many have been attending this County Fair all their lives, since they were kids, since the time when Jimmie Guptil, aged six, won first prize for a golden Hubbard's squash that weighed over 150 pounds, and Teresa Pinch, aged seven, won a prize for a towel, that had cross-stitched on it the motto of the Women's Institute, "For Home and Country." As grown men and women, they've never outlived the pride of that unbelievable, shimmering moment when they were handed a ribbon and told that they were Number One.

They keep coming back every year. All through those years, during Exhibition Week, they've been meeting the rest of this family from all over the county. Pretty soon, Jimmie Guptil and Teresa Pinch are observed wandering about the midway, eating candied apples— which is difficult enough to do when you're walking hand-in-hand....

These are people who meet once a year...to take a good look at themselves and to learn from each other, such things as how to fix those brass tips onto the end of the oxen's horns, the way to make homemade bread that wins a blue ribbon (information available only to special friends), or how to piece together a prize-winning patchwork quilt.

You learn that many of the farmers come to these fairs in trailers and live here all week, in a little trailer village at the side of the park.

Here they visit back and forth, talking over the day's events—the ten-man tug-of-war teams, the horse-jumping competition, and the special charms of the poultry house, with its pouter pigeons, banty roosters, and exotic varieties of ducks and geese. There is always something new and interesting to discuss.

These people are all friends, with whom they can perhaps share a quiet nip from a flask, if the wife happens to be helping out at the fried chicken stand of the Ladies' Hospital Auxiliary.

The lowest income in Canada? I wonder. It could be that these people enjoy more genuine security and greater wealth—the lasting wealth of human companionship—than even those high-priced statisticians in Ottawa.

◆

*Ox-pull,
Avonport, N.S.*

The Uncertainties of Politics

"...that lighted lantern is remembered..."

We have some elections coming up in New Brunswick and P.E.I. and, as with every election, as we draw closer to election day, each political party grows more and more confident that they will be the winner. It is part of the electioneering process designed to persuade us to board the bandwagon and vote for the victor. But, in reality, only the electorate knows how the election will turn out and the electorate is saying nothing.

In the provincial election of 1948, every newspaper across the United States was predicting a victory for Governor Thomas E. Dewey. They even came out with headlines the day after election day saying he'd won, whereas, in fact, he'd lost to the underdog, Harry S. Truman. You never can tell about elections until the votes are counted.

In September of 1866, the *Charlottetown Islander* had this to say: *There is not the slightest chance of Confederation being accepted by the people of Prince Edward Island.* Seven years later, Islanders decided to give it a try.

Another island—Surrette's Island in Yarmouth County, N.S.—wasn't sure if *it* wanted to join the mainland, in this case with a bridge. Some wanted the bridge; others didn't. About 1900, the bridge to Surrettes Island became a political issue in that part of Yarmouth County known as The Argyles. Those who opposed the bridge said so on election day but, in due time, the bridge got built. Over the years that bridge provided not only safe passage to and from Surrette's Island but a weather forecast as well. At nightfall, whenever the residents of Argyle could hear the sound of a car passing over the bridge they would say, "Tomorrow it'll be a fine day." And it always was.

So, although they may have lost the election, they gained a bridge along with its built-in barometer.

Not so happy was the outcome of the federal election of 1908, in Sandy Cove in Digby County, N.S. The Liberals had won the seat in the House of Commons. Their man in Digby County was A.J.S. Copp. When news of his victory reached Sandy Cove, his jubilant supporters strung a banner across the main street bearing these words of triumph: Hurrah for Copp. Not everyone in Sandy Cove was pleased with that banner—certainly not Dr. Morse, the Baptist minister, or Dr. Rice, or Fred Sypher, all good Conservatives. In fact, Dr. Rice made his displeasure known by refusing to drive his horse and buggy under the banner. He would get out of his carriage and lead his horse down into the ditch rather than pass under those exultant and gleeful words.

Two years later, in another federal election, the Conservatives had their chance to crow when Robert L. Borden, from the Annapolis Valley, confounded the pollsters by defeating the great Sir Wilfred Laurier and becoming Prime Minister of Canada. That upset victory of 1911 was celebrated in a very special way in the little village of Morell, on P.E.I, along the coast from Stanhope, Brackley Beach and Savage Harbour. A girl by the name of Eppie Leslie, who lived with her family on the family farm on Mount Mary, lighted a lantern that night, the night of the 1911 election. (This was long before electricity came to that part of the Island.) Taking the lantern with her, Eppie climbed to the top of a windmill that stood in the yard of her father's farm and fastened the lantern to the very top of the windmill. As news of Borden's victory spread throughout the countryside, a strange light appeared in the night sky, north-west of the village. That lighted lantern of the young girl, Eppie Leslie, is remembered today in the village of Morell.

In 1920, Nova Scotia held a provincial election which had a most unexpected outcome. Until that time there had been just the two parties to vote for. You elected either a Liberal or a Conservative. That's the way it always had been and always would be, but, once again, the electors had other ideas.

This was the first election since the Canadian Army had returned from overseas. It was also the first election since women had been given the right to vote. Many, both men and women, seized the occasion to express opposition to the old-line parties.

A party was formed representing the United Farmers. They joined forces with various labour groups in Pictou, Cape Breton, and Halifax. The outcome left the old-line parties completely bewildered. Across Nova Scotia, some eleven Farmer-Labour candidates were elected. They even out-polled the Tories and formed the official opposition. It was the most surprising upset that had ever happened in Nova Scotia politics.

Although the Conservatives lost, they scored a moral victory in being the first party to nominate a woman candidate—Mrs. Grace McLeod Rogers, author of several books on Maritime history, and wife of Amherst lawyer, H. Wyckoff Rogers. Mrs. Rogers did not win, but she topped her eight male competitors at two of the polls—and led all conservative candidates in Cumberland county.

That was not bad for an election in the year 1920. It just shows that, when it comes to elections, you never can tell who is going to win.

THE WAYWARD BLACKBERRY

I like to think I am a careful sort of person—careful about things like not walking on the grass in the Public Gardens and always remembering to drop empty gum wrappers in the trash can, things like that. Ever since they posted a notice on the window of our Town Hall, making the use of firecrackers a punishable offence, I haven't set off one firecracker inside the town limits. I'm that kind. I'm very law-abiding.

I suppose it's partly respect for authority, and partly because I can't bear to see things being destroyed or going to waste.

I just wanted to put in that little personal note so you would understand how I felt about these blackberries. We'd never had such a crop. They hung on the bushes in great clusters, ripening in the autumn sunshine. The brambles had spread all the way from my bee hives to the wild crabapple tree. Almost everyone in our town has a back lot, with plum trees, and pears, a kitchen garden, a grape arbour...and one corner where the blackberry canes have got beyond control. Now in September, what with wild aster, and golden rod, and Queen Anne's lace, it's as pretty a spot as you'll find on the property.

In other years I had tried to keep the brambles mowed down with a bush scythe; but as they always grew up again, its seemed a waste of energy—and, as I say, I hate waste. That is why we have a hammock out under the big maple; you can save all kinds of energy while lying in that hammock.

It also gives you a good view of the blackberry patch. The sight of those brambles, dripping with fruit, and no one bothering to pick them, was a sore trial to me. Finally, they took to dropping off the bushes and I had to choose between saving the blackberries...or some more energy.

I picked two big pails, rounding-full. Then I sat down to figure out what I'd do with them. It was no use offering them to the neighbours; they all had blackberries of their own. So I looked through the cookbook, to see what a person could *make* with blackberries.

There was jam or jelly—the kind of thing where they get you over a hot stove "stirring constantly." After I had been stirring for upwards of an hour, I wanted to get back to the hammock. These recipes really didn't appeal to me. I kept on hunting through the cookbook, and at last came on precisely what I was looking for—and in the strangest place, under the section marked Beverages. It was a drink, called Blackberry Lemonade.

Here is how it's made. You put the black-berries in a bowl, pour some boiling water over them, enough to cover—about a gallon of water to a gallon of fruit. Then you leave it there for three days while you save your energy in the hammock, and then you press out the juice by straining it through a piece of cheesecloth. Finally, (and this is most important) you add the juice of a lemon... just one.

Now, that sounds easy enough, doesn't it? Because of this disarming simplicity, I grew overconfident—indeed neglectful. By the time I remembered to strain out the juice, a change had taken place. I noticed it the moment I stepped into the pantry. You could *hear* something...a faint crackling noise. The juice was beginning to bubble.

I dipped a spoon in and took a sip. It had developed the oddest flavour—a sort of sharp taste. I don't know just how to describe it. It wasn't the lemon; it was something else. The juice wasn't quite as sweet as it had been. Apparently the bubbling was affecting it.

Well, I was pretty upset, I can tell you that. All those luscious blackberries—and *now* look what's happening. Nobody would want to drink it if it was going to turn sour.

So I decided I'd better add some sugar. I added sugar—three pounds to the gallon. It did no good, only made it bubble worse than ever. That is when I got the idea of putting it into bottles. The bubbling would have to stop if I kept the air from getting at it.

I bottled it, and drove some good tight corks into the necks of the bottles so no air could get in. As I was a little uncertain as to what might happen next, I set the bottles in a place where I could keep an eye on them. The most convenient place seemed to be behind the kitchen stove.

That evening, two neighbours dropped in and I entertained them in the front room. Excusing myself, I retired to the kitchen to prepare refreshments—a glass of ginger ale and some cookies—and was on the point of returning with the tray, when a loud report echoed through the house. A cork bounced off the kitchen stove. I had scarcely recovered from my alarm, when two more corks hit the ceiling almost simultaneously, like a twelve gauge shotgun, blazing with both barrels.

On rejoining my guests I could see the look of inquiry in their eyes...but I said nothing. What *could* I say? How was I to explain away a thing like that? Oh, I could have told them the truth—that I was making blackberry lem-onade, but do you suppose they would have believed me? Of course not.

After they left, I stood by the grate, staring into the fire, trying to understand how this horrible thing had happened to me. I could almost hear them telling the news around town, going on about the sound they had heard, like the crack of a rifle shot...and me offering no word of explanation. What had I got myself into? After all, there is a law against the illegal possession of firearms. If they spread a report that I had a twenty-two repeater, without a permit.... That night I hardly slept a wink. My bedroom is directly over the kitchen stove.

It would be no use going to the police. They couldn't give me a permit for a gun I didn't have and I knew very well they wouldn't be interested in a bottle that shot corks.

It looked as if there was only one way out... down the kitchen sink. And yet, I couldn't bring myself to do it. The thought of all those ripe blackberries, and all that good sugar, and that lemon. Why throw it away? It was perfectly all right. There was nothing wrong with it—except the corks pop out now and then. Maybe they'll get over that after awhile. I put the corks back in, and then I covered all the bottles with an apple barrel, to catch the next volley.

But no matter how well I muffled them, my sleep was still troubled. Even in my dreams I could hear those corks popping—sometimes like distant field artillery, at other times like an old-fashioned muzzle-loader. If only it hadn't been October, of all months, because you know how strict the authorities are about

"Even in my dreams I could hear those corks popping–"

people using guns during the hunting season!

With the coming of frost, the popping gradually subsided, but this was to prove only a temporary truce. With the arrival of Indian Summer, our kitchen was like a frontier blockhouse under attack.

It was with a sense of relief that I marked the approach of Yuletide. Here was an opportunity to rid myself of these disturbers of the peace and also, to come up with an inexpensive solution to my Christmas shopping.

I don't know how *you* feel about present-giving...but it always seems to me that a present you make yourself has a value above anything you buy—a certain intangible something. I was optimistic enough to hope that in these bottles of mine there might be this certain intangible something. I wrapped each bottle up in coloured tinfoil, to make it a gay holiday package, and on the twenty-fourth of December, I loaded up a basket and started out on my rounds. I gave a bottle to each of my friends and wished them all a merry Christmas. So that is how I came to make blackberry lemonade. Do you know, my friends tell me it's really quite good.

◆

AMATEUR WEATHER FORECASTING

Some years ago I had a touch of arthritis. Now there is nothing very pleasant about arthritis. It can be excruciatingly painful, and offers only one redeeming advantage. It allows you to predict the weather.

When my arthritis finally went away, it did so for no good reason that I could see as I hadn't taken any special treatment for it. It just stopped bothering me and one day it was gone. When it had left me, I found that I could no longer tell what the weather was going to be.

You know, I began to miss it just a little. After you have enjoyed the privilege of a built-in weather bureau, it's hard to resign yourself to being made of common clay, without so much as a twinge to warn you of approaching rain.

Then I began to notice something. I noticed that some of my neighbours were able to predict the weather even though they didn't have arthritis and I became interested in trying to find out how they did it. Here are some of the things I learned.

"...allows you to predict the weather."

One of the most useful household barometers is a pot of boiling potatoes. If the potatoes boil dry it means we're in for wet weather. The weather-wise housewife can then serve up dinner along with a storm warning, "Now George, I don't want to hear one word about the potatoes tasting burnt. They boiled dry, so you put your rubbers on this afternoon. We'll have rain for sure."

Another sign of approaching rain is when you see the soot or creosote at the back of a fireplace beginning to burn, or glow, moving across the bricks like an army of red-coated soldiers. The old folks used to speak of these little patches of burning soot as "the red coats," and they looked on it as an infallible sign. I had an old aunt who loved to sit beside the fireplace and sweep up the hearth and watch the wood burning. Whenever she saw that little army of redcoats, breaking out into a gallop on the sooty bricks, marching up the chimney, their banners aflame, she was sure that we were in for bad weather. She was generally right.

While we're talking about fireplaces, the draft is always twice as good when the wind is from the nor'west which is very fortunate because, in the wintertime, our prevailing wind here in the Maritimes is from this direction—the northwest.

A south wind has a depressing effect on the draft. If you watch the smoke coming out of the chimney, you'll notice that when the wind is from the south, the smoke blows down over the roof. If it is a one-storey house, the smoke will sometimes blow right down on the ground. That means we're in for damp weather. When the smoke goes straight up in the air we can expect fine weather.

Everyone knows that when the wind is from the East...it is fit for neither man nor beast. It is a peculiar thing about pigs, but the harder the wind blows, the louder they squeal. They seem to sense that wind is likely to mean trouble.

Seagulls can even anticipate a wind. When you see the gulls flying overland in large numbers, particularly if they are flying high, that is a sign of wind coming.

Now we today don't have to worry about the wind the way they did 60 or 70 years ago, when every second or third home had a man away at sea in ships that depended on the wind as their means of locomotion. The old sailor-men developed a very keen awareness of any-

thing that might help them in their prognostications, and this was especially true of the skipper. On those old windjammers, the ship's master spent most of his time studying the clouds, watching the sea gulls, observing a school of porpoise. Any of these things might tell him what to expect. He kept a careful record of barometric readings, and he balanced this primitive science against the weather lore which he carried about in his head.

An old friend of mine who used to go to sea has helped me picture just what it would be like on the bridge of one of those sailing ships.

It is morning. The captain has just come out on deck. He stands with the mate, scanning the heavens.

Well, I don't like it. I don't like the look of that mackerel sky one bit. See those mares' tails over there. You know the old saying: Mackerel skies and mares' tails make lofty ships carry light sails. That wind is liable to blow up a gale any minute. We've got to get some of this stuff off her quick before it strikes. Take the topsails off, haul that mainsail in and put a reef in him. Put a reef in the spanker, and take in the standing and staysail jibs. Then you'll have just the one full sail, the foresail, and then you got her in your fingers. We have to get trimmed down quick. Look at those seagulls. Get the men aloft now, she's startin' to bend.

They would get the sails trimmed down, and ride out the storm. A week later, they'd be lying becalmed, praying for wind.

Wind can be a dangerous thing even on land. I know a place down in Cape Breton, near Margaree Harbour, where at certain times of the year they have sudden, violent windstorms—so violent, in fact, that some of the buildings have to be anchored down with guy wires pegged to the ground, to keep them from blowing away. It has something to do with the air currents around those rolling Cape Breton hills. It is far too local a phenomenon for the weather bureau to take note of, and yet, for the people living there, it could be quite serious. No doubt they look for certain signs to warn them of the coming of these winds.

There are other local phenomena which can help in weather prediction. For example, in the vicinity of Minas Basin, there are certain days when Cape Blomidon looms up as if it were only half the distance away, when you can look across the Basin to the blue Parrsboro hills and make out the red cliffs and the fields lying back of them, and almost imagine you see the teams at work haying. Five Islands is so distinct that you can count each separate island—all five of them. On such a morning, you will hear the train whistling away up the line. A robin is trilling a strange lonely little song which he sings only on such mornings as this. Everything is sparkling clear, the river like glass and the reflections of the opposite shore float on the water like a picture. Across the river, you can hear a dog barking. What does it all mean? A storm is brewing.

When the sun rises behind a streak of clouds and then bursts out into the clear, then you are going to have a fine day. Also, when the sun sets in a clear sky, it is a pretty good indication of a fine day tomorrow.

Cape Blomidon, N.S.

Oh yes, and after a storm, in the afternoon, if the clouds break in the westward, and you can see enough blue sky to make a Dutchman a pair of pants, it's a sure sign of clearing weather.

As for fog —well, fog on the hill gives you water for the mill. Fog in the hollow, clear, cool weather to follow. This simply means that high fog brings rain, and low fog brings cool weather. This may perhaps apply only to the Annapolis Valley, where the fogs generally come no further than the top of the North Mountain.

What other things have my neighbours taught me about the weather? If it is one of those rainy, splashy, slushy days, a really dirty day, you'll have no shaving problem. Your beard will cut as easily as June grass on a dewy morning. Your car, when you step on the accelerator, will be in tip-top shape. For some mysterious reason, the motor will have more power on one of these drizzly, miserable mornings.

But if you are a woman, wet weather seems sent to try the soul, with table salt that cakes together, and soot that falls down over the house and blows in the window, hair that becomes unruly, and five dollar permanents that disappear overnight.

But cheer up! There is one thing you won't have to worry about. The potatoes are not going to boil dry.

◆

THE SAXBY GALE

In December of 1868, Lieutenant S. M. Saxby, a young officer in the Royal Navy and an earnest student of astronomy, wrote to the *London Times* warning that in October of the coming year would occur a gale of immense and devastating force. Lieutenant Saxby even foretold the day—October 5.

He did not, however, say where this gale would strike. And since gales are quite common in October, it was not such a remarkable prediction that a gale of some sort would turn up somewhere in the world.

However, Lieutenant Saxby did spell out very clearly that this particular gale would prove to be extremely destructive. In this part of his prediction...he was right.

A great gale did occur, the Saxby gale, on the night of October 4 and 5, 1869, just as he said it would. It was the worst gale ever seen in the Maritime provinces, for this is where it happened.

Those who had read Lieutenant Saxby's prediction—and it was widely published in newspapers on this continent—dismissed the warning as so much alarmist talk...like that which said the world was coming to an end.

Certainly the weather gave no cause for uneasiness. October 4 dawned without the slightest sign of anything unusual or foreboding. Along the New Brunswick coast, from St. Stephen to Saint John, water lapped lazily against the wharf pilings under a blanket of

Cape Blomidon and Parrsboro, N.S. from a Bartlett print.

"...you could hear the waves beginning to boom..."

fog, which later cleared, giving way to a warm sunny morning. It was a perfect autumn day.

Then about noon, at the entrance to Yarmouth Harbour, N.S., whitecaps began to appear, as a light breeze from the southwest gathered strength. As the afternoon advanced, the breeze increased steadily and the heat became oppressive. Out by Yarmouth lighthouse, or at The Churn, on the way to Cape Forchu, you could hear the waves beginning to boom, and the Michaelmas daisies were wet with spindrift. Toward the south, the sky loomed dull and leaded, growing darker as the afternoon wore on, with the rising wind riding the sky on a witch's broom of scudding storm clouds. By five o'clock the wind reached hurricane force. By six, trees were falling as if felled by an axe. By nine o'clock, the raging, terrifying Saxby Gale was at its height.

We can have no idea today how terrifying this gale must have seemed to people cut off and alone, with no means of communicating with their neighbours. There was no telephone, no electric light to snap on. Many homes were without even a kerosene lamp, and it was hard enough to keep a candle alight in the drafty houses.

One man described it like this:

The extreme darkness, the constant roar and tumult of wind, the lashing rain, the groaning of great trees, the hail of debris, shingles, branches, objects large and small falling everywhere, roofs carried aloft, whole buildings collapsing, all gave a paralysing sense of insecurity and calamity.

And now, they began to recall Lieutenant Saxby and his prediction...and they wondered if it was to grow even worse.

In New Brunswick, at St. Andrews, 123 vessels were tossed up onto the beach. A barque was sunk at Lepreau with a loss of 11 lives. On Campobello Island wind and tide destroyed over 80 buildings. The roof of the Volunteer Armoury in St. George was carried 100 yards by the wind. In St. Stephen a man was picked up by the wind, carried across the street, and deposited on the other sidewalk.

As the gale raced up the Bay of Fundy it swept the water on ahead and forced it into the inner reaches of the bay—into Shepody Bay and Cumberland Basin and Minas Basin.

In the town of Annapolis, N.S., water was knee-deep on lower St. George Street. At Grand Pré it breached the Great Horton Dyke, flooding 3,000 acres and drowning many head of cattle.

At Moncton the tide rose nine feet over the Harris wharf at the foot of South King Street, and up onto the warehouses, destroying a quantity of salt, flour and other perishables. A mark was notched on the side of one of the warehouses to show the height of the tide. If you are ever driving through Moncton you can see a similar marker at Boreview Park, along with a plaque indicating the height of the tide at just before midnight on the fateful evening of October 4, 1869.

At Coverdale, near Moncton, N.B., Jacob and Ellen O'Brien and their six children were sleeping when the noise of the gale awakened the parents. Although it was pitch black outside they could hear the swirling water as the tide rose around their house. They built a flimsy raft out of fence rails and kindling wood. The parents entered the water and placed the children on the raft, attempting to direct it.

The gale blew them across the river to the Westmorland County side, and the children were washed away from the raft...one by one.

But the greatest destruction of all took place on the Tantramar Marshes on the border between Nova Scotia and New Brunswick. Cattle and sheep were still out at pasture. As the wind rose to gale force, they huddled in the lee of the many hay stacks and hay barns that dotted the marshes. Their owners felt that at least the animals were safe, protected by the outer dykes which were 25 feet high.

One of these owners was Charles Stewart of Minudie, an elderly Scotsman who had emigrated to Nova Scotia and taken up land in the Joggins-Lower Cove district, at the head of Chignecto Bay.

On the afternoon of the fourth, before the wind blew up, Charles Stewart had decided to make a trip out to his hay barn on the marshes. His team consisted of a mare with a colt by her side. Because of the colt, and because Mr. Stewart was a kindly old man who didn't overdrive his animals, they made slow progress. By the time he had the hay cart loaded, it was growing dark and the wind had come up. Mr. Stewart decided to stay the night in the hay barn where he bedded down among the hay, tethering the mare and her colt to the outside of the barn.

What Charles Stewart did not know was that the tide had risen above those outer dykes, that the dykes were crumbling, and that within a short time a great tidal wave would sweep in over the Tantramar Marshes, carrying before it a churning flotsam of hay barns and hay stacks and struggling animals.

The water soon surrounded his barn and he might well have gone on sleeping, quite unaware of what was happening, if the little colt had not set up a great clamour of alarm, whinnying to its mother.

Stewart leaped down from the hayloft and found himself waist-deep in water. Struggling in the dark he managed to untie the mare, climb on her back, and start for home, leading the colt by a lead line around its neck. They were soon in water many feet deep; the tide had turned and was ebbing with tremendous force and the mare was quite unable to swim against it. Carried along by the tide, Stewart clung to her back, while trying to tow the colt by the lead line, but in the rushing water the colt was torn from his grasp and swept away into the darkness and tumult of the night.

The mare, with Stewart holding on fast, finally brought up against a dyke lining the edge of the marsh, and there they held on till daylight, when they made their way back to the home farm.

Only then, did Charles Stewart realize that the dykes had broken, that the marshes were completely flooded—even the streets in the town of Amherst. Barns and hay stacks had been floated off their foundations, and the dead bodies of hundreds of animals littered the marshes.

Charles Stewart owed his life to his horse and the colt who had warned him of approaching danger.

For this account of Charles Stewart and his night on the marsh, I am indebted to a correspondent in Parrsboro, Miss M. B. Morwick, who heard the story from Mr. Stewart's grandson.

There you have some of the things that happened during the Saxby Gale of October 4 and 5, 1869. It was the greatest gale the Maritimes has ever seen. ◆

"...the tide had turned and was ebbing with tremendous force..."

THANKSGIVING

For those of us who live here in Nova Scotia—or in any of Canada's Atlantic Provinces, for that matter—our national holiday of Thanksgiving has a very special meaning. We are essentially a rural people in this part of Canada, still fairly close to the soil. And this celebration we call Thanksgiving is simply a harvest festival.

Anyone who has ever had a garden, and has watched the corn tassels change colour, or the squash vine blackening under the first touch of frost, must feel a kind of reverence in the presence of the natural forces of nature. Even those who dwell in the city, do their shopping at the supermarket, and never get any closer to a garden than a package of corn flakes, must rely on the rich bounty of Mother Earth. And here, in Canada's Atlantic Provinces, we have the sea as well to provide us with its own teeming harvest.

We are very fortunate people here in the Maritimes. Sometimes we grumble. Sometimes we feel we are not receiving as much of this world's goods as those in other parts of Canada. Sometimes we leave home and seek our fortune in a strange city—in Toronto, in Montreal, in Boston, or New York. Only then do we realize how generously nature has favoured the folks back home, on the little side-hill farm, or in some fisherman's cottage

"...when it comes time to decorate the church for the harvest festival..."

on a lonely headland. The air is so clean. The fields are still hospitable to a man with a dog sniffing out the pheasants that rise with a clatter of wings. Very few signs read: Private—Keep Out. We still enjoy the freedom to explore the woods, and to pick wild cranberries on the margin of a secluded lake. We are still very close to the fundamentals.

"We grow our own vegetables."

In the little town where I live, in Nova Scotia's Annapolis Valley, most of us have a garden. We grow our own vegetables. It gives us an opportunity to share some of our surplus with the neighbours, who have no cucumber bed, or had poor luck with their tomatoes. We take a certain pride in showing some of this produce at the county exhibition, and when it comes time to decorate the church for the harvest festival, we participate in a very intimate way in this special service of Thanksgiving.

On Saturday afternoon, the cars begin to gather at the church. Boxes and cartons are carried into the vestibule. Vegetables and fruit and flowers are banked up around the chancel steps, the lectern, and the pulpit. The foot of the font is glowing with cosmos and wild aster. In the corners of the church stand stalks of corn, and along the window ledges among the autumn leaves are bottles of pickles and damson plums. All of this is grown or pro-duced by members of the church. On the altar is a loaf of home-made bread and a bunch of home-grown purple grapes.

At the service on Sunday, the congregation rises to sing the old Thanksgiving hymns, "We Plow the Fields and Scatter," and "Come Ye Thankful People, Come." For those of us who still have gardens, they have their own personal meaning.

Next morning, the ladies of the church are busy packing up all the fruits and vegetables, getting them ready to send to the hospital. It used to be that the minister accepted these things as a tribute from his flock, because ministers were not very well off and often had a large family to feed. Sometimes they were distributed among the poor, to homes where the men were out of work. Today, we have no poor families in our town, so we send these offerings to the hospital. Yes, I think we have much to be thankful for.

◆

Editor's Note: This piece pre-dates Food Banks in Nova Scotia.

It's Time to
Have Your Chimney Cleaned

Leaning chimney at Nova Scotia Textiles Ltd., Windsor, N.S.

In the summer of 1973, two young men in the Vermont resort town of Stowe, found themselves running out of work. They had been house painting most of the summer, but now, with September approaching, the summer visitors were packing up and going back to the city. The lights were going out in one house after another. As the lights disappeared, so did the jobs, as in so many resort towns here in the Maritimes.

Well, these two young men did not want to leave the town of Stowe. They enjoyed the more leisurely life-style in Vermont—if only they could find some work in the fall and spring of the year when the tourists weren't in town.

One day, an old Vermonter whose house they were painting happened to mention that he had dropped a chain down his flue and it had landed on the smoke shelf. They had no idea what he was talking about, but he went on complaining that every fall he had to clean his chimney...because there weren't any chimney sweeps around the country like there used to be.

This gave our two young men an idea. More and more Vermonters were installing wood stoves, cutting stove wood, if they had a woodlot, or buying it. Burning wood was one way of making sure you would not freeze in the dark. So, with all these wood stoves sending smoke up the chimneys, maybe this was a good time to take up chimney sweeping.

This is exactly what they did. They knew absolutely nothing about sweeping chimneys when they started out, but they kept making inquiries, and learning by experience. People would tell them how the chimneys used to be cleaned. Some householders had cleaned their own chimneys, sometimes by swinging a chain around in the flue, or pulling a small tree up and down the chimney. Others would fill a burlap bag with bricks and lower it down the chimney. They also heard of another method—which they did not condone—tying a goose by the feet and lowering him into the flue to beat the creosote off with his wings.

Then somebody gave them two old top hats and two sets of tails so at least they

"...somebody gave them...top hats... so at least they looked like chimney sweeps."

looked like chimney sweeps. Cleaning their first chimney took them more than three hours and left them filthy, their lungs filled with soot. Today, seven years later, these two young men can clean a chimney in a little over half an hour, hardly soiling their hands, and have made themselves a nice little business.

A few weeks ago I sent away for their catalogue, and no sooner opened it, than I found myself swept into this magic world of chimney sweeping. This is a fast-growing profession. One can attend workshops, and with proper equipment and training can sweep a chimney in an hour or less.

Then you can be your own boss—choose your own hours, take vacations when you want, decide how hard you want to work and how much money you make. Your hot water bill will go up of course....

Here in the catalogue is a picture of me wearing top-hat and tails (something I've never been able to afford). They say every professional sweep needs at least one set of tails, and a top quality top hat is a must.

It sounds like the answer to a dream—sweeping chimneys. Why haven't I thought of it before? I can hardly wait to get started. I'll be seeing you—up on the roof.

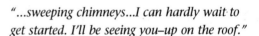

"...sweeping chimneys...I can hardly wait to get started. I'll be seeing you–up on the roof."

MISS SHAND'S WEDDING DRESS

"...the dressmaker stayed up quite late..."

In the early part of October in the year 1897, Miss Florence Shand of Windsor, N.S., sent out some wedding invitations, announcing her forthcoming marriage to Dr. Bret Black, also of Windsor, whose father was the member of parliament for Hants County. The ceremony was to take place on Wednesday, October 20.

It promised to be one of the social events of the season. The Shands were an old and respected Windsor family. The finest taffeta had been obtained for Florence's wedding gown, which was being made by a local dressmaker. At that time, in 1897, Windsor had its wide porticoes and spacious drawing rooms, resting on the profits of ship-building and ship-owning. Neat white picket fences lined the sidewalks. The dusty streets dreamed under the shade of wine-glass elms, some of them planted as far back as 1764 when this little port on the Avon River had been granted the status of a township.

The wedding, as I say, was to take place on Wednesday, October 20. One final fitting remained to be taken care of. Four days before the wedding, on Saturday, the gown was almost finished—in fact, the dressmaker stayed up quite late that Saturday night, stitching by the light of an oil lamp.

The dressmaker lived on Gerrish Street, about a block away from the Court House and not far from the fire hall where they kept the horse-drawn fire engine and the hose-reels which, in those days, were hauled along the street by the firemen themselves. When, shortly after midnight the bell in the fire hall began to ring, she went to the window and looked out. A wind was stirring the dust on Gerrish Street. It rattled the window, and she noticed that dry leaves were swirling about the eaves of the house. They rose up to the roof-tops, where some of them were caught under the dog-eared shingles of the older houses.

From several directions footsteps were heard as men came running toward the fire hall and within a few minutes a hose-reel, drawn by six men, went rattling off downtown toward Water Street and disappeared in a cloud of dust.

A fire had broken out on the waterfront. Smoke streamed from a dockside warehouse.

Inside, an ugly glow boiled and fretted at the windows. Someone smashed in a window-pane and flames shot up over the roof, lighting up the masts and rigging of ships lying at the wharves. The firemen worked frantically, unwinding the hose-reels and connecting the hose to a fire hydrant.

At that time Windsor had a water pressure of 90 pounds, which was quite sufficient for normal fire-fighting. But this fire, fanned by a gale force wind, created such intense heat that the men were driven back to another hydrant, without having had a chance to turn off the first hydrant. This of course reduced the water pressure. The fire soon spread to other buildings, most of them wooden, and the men fell back to a third hydrant. By this time the pressure had sunk to a point where the hoses were almost useless.

If this fire occurred today, even with a stiff autumn gale, it would not get out of hand. Fire Chief Walter Stephens tells me that back in 1897 the Windsor Fire Department had only 500 feet of hose. Today they have over a mile of hose in addition to ten pieces of motorised equipment, including an 85-foot aerial ladder and four triple-combination pumpers.

Back in 1897 there was nothing but the horse-drawn fire engine and the hose-reels. Within an hour the fire was hopelessly out of control.

Burning shingles soared up into the night sky and scattered across the town. Sparks fell like Roman candles and smouldered on the tinder-dry roofs. The firemen ran through the streets, pounding on doors and calling out to the owners that their houses were on fire.

People stumbled from their burning homes with nothing on but a nightgown. A few had time to tie up some valuables in a sheet, or lug some cherished piece of furniture out onto the street. Some carried their belongings up to higher ground on Fort Edward; but even here the sparks fell and furnishings that had been dragged to safety caught fire and were left marred and disfigured.

One old man, who had brought a blanket from the house to keep himself warm, now looked back on the roaring town below and saw the flames beginning to creep up over the roof of his house. He pulled the blanket over his head and would look no more.

"...Miss Shand's family... home was one of the few that had been spared."

Old Mr. John Keith on Clifton Avenue stood dazed as the firemen began carrying furniture from his house. All he could think of to say, as the house burned down, was, "Careful, boys. Watch out for the woodwork. Don't scratch the paint."

Inside Christ Church its rector, Canon Maynard, was praying—praying that the flames would stop before they reached the King Street intersection. At the same moment, boys from Kings Collegiate were up on the roof of Christ Church emptying buckets of water. Between Canon Maynard's prayers and the buckets of water the church was saved. It was the only church in Windsor not reduced to ashes.

Miss Shand's dressmaker, meanwhile, standing at her window, watched the houses on the other side of the street, as flames began to trickle along the leaf-filled gutters. From the roof of her own house came the crackling of shingles. She looked hastily about the room, snatched up the wedding dress, and ran out into the streets.

Flying embers were everywhere. It needed only one stray spark, and this dress, on which she had lavished her best skill, would be damaged beyond use.

A light was on in the Court House. Not the light of something burning out of control, this was the steady glow of a lamp. Someone was in the building. Through the smoke and tumult of the streets, she made her way up to the Court House, pushed open the door, and burst in on the County Sheriff who was running about gathering up records and documents and storing them away in the big walk-in vault—the biggest vault in town.

She thrust the wedding dress into his hands and asked that it be given the protection of the Court House vault. And that is how Miss Shand's wedding dress came to be one of the few things that survived the Windsor fire.

But what about the wedding? The fire continued burning all that night and all through the next day, which was Sunday, October 17. The wedding was to be on the Wednesday. At first it was thought best to call it off. But for how long? Until Windsor was rebuilt?

The entire town had been destroyed by this fire, with the exception of a few homes on the outskirts of the town and a section near the bridge known as Ferry Hill.

It so happened that Miss Shand's family lived on Ferry Hill. Their home was one of the few that had been spared. Since the home was still available and the wedding dress had been saved, why not go ahead with the wedding? Besides, the invitations had already been mailed out, and there was no longer a post-office through which to advise the guests that the affair was to be postponed. So it was decided to go ahead with the wedding.

It was a strange setting for a wedding. Red-coated soldiers from Halifax, toting muskets, patrolled the streets to prevent the looting of furniture, and watched over the smoking ruins. Most people had laid in their winter's supply of coal, and this still glowed and smouldered in the cellars.

The Court House had been burned to the ground. Nothing was left standing but the vault, which remained so hot that the officials refused to open it. They feared that the paper contents might burst into flames. Even by Wednesday, three days after the fire, the vault was still warm to the touch.

So Miss Shand was not married in her wedding dress after all. Instead, she wore a purple velvet dress from her trousseau which looked perfectly all right because the guests came in the most oddly assorted costumes. Most of them had escaped from their homes with nothing but the clothes they were wearing and sometimes that was only a nightgown. But the strange costumes became, for these Windsor folk, a source of merriment. They pointed out the ill-matched shoes; the dress that was pock-marked where the sparks had fallen; the trousers that didn't fit. These people who had lost so much found something to laugh about on that wedding day.

◆

Windsor, N.S. the day after the 1897 fire.

Headless Men and Ghostly Lights

"...there is the ghost of an old lady...in a rocking chair...and she, also, has no head."

You can't live on Prince Edward Island for too many years without establishing friendly relations with a fair number of ghosts. They have all kinds of ghosts on the Island. I guess they used to scare people but today, whether at Hallowe'en or other times, if the folks at Clyde River walk along the road toward the Clyde River Bridge they would be disappointed if they didn't see a dim wavering light drifting slowly up the hill, past the Presbyterian church, to a point near the Bannockburn Road where, after a tantalizing pause, it fades from view.

Don't be alarmed. It's a forerunner, of course. But the calamities it foretells nowadays are not much worse than inflation or rising grocery bills. If we didn't have a dim wavering light of some sort, Hallowe'en would be kind of tame.

Also on P.E.I., beyond New Haven Corner, where Cameron Road branches off towards the river, is the haunt of Artie Webster's ghost. Artie Webster was an itinerant preacher who was killed here when he fell from the old white horse on which he always travelled on his preaching trips about the Island. (Did you notice he used a white horse? That was thoughtful of him.) It was thoughtful, too, to have fallen off his horse on this very night—Hallowe'en. So tonight, if you go a little beyond New Haven Corner, after dark, of course, you'll see Artie Webster's ghost astride a white horse on his way to keep his yearly appointment at the crossroads.

Then there is the murder at Goblin Hollow, near Lyndale, not too many miles from the Island community of Orwell. *That* was really frightening. I would not blame the kids of Lyndale if they stayed in at Hallowe'en, or started out on their rounds with garbage bags and Unicef boxes before the sun went down, because a certain spot in Lyndale is haunted by the ghost of Ann Beaton. She was most foully murdered in the year 1859, clubbed to death with a grubbing hoe. It is part of the folklore of P.E.I. "The Ballad of Ann Beaton" is a song written about this event which happened in Goblin Hollow.

For years after this murder, it was said around Lyndale, that a woman would not go out in the dark to take her drying clothes in

off the line, and any man who had to visit his barn on a moonless night would awaken a child from sleep...to keep him company.

Goblin Hollow became a sort of test for the boys of Lyndale. While it was still broad daylight they would make a trip to the spot where this murder had occurred. They would tie to a tree a handkerchief in which a penny had been hidden. That night, whether there was a moon or not, any boy courageous enough to go to the tree and recover the handkerchief could claim ownership of the penny.

Goblin Hollow is one of many places on the Island where haunts and ghostly sightings provide a chilling brush with the supernatural.

Now in case you are new to this part of Canada and find these ghost stories intimidating, don't worry. For the most part, they are only stories—something that was told to a *very* trustworthy friend of yours, who would never think of telling a lie. In almost every case, he didn't actually see these things himself, he only heard about them. Sir Walter Scott, in his fascinating book on Demonology and Witchcraft, tells about a judge in an English court who was officiating at a murder trial.

One witness gave him an account of the murder as narrated to him by the ghost of the murdered person.

"Hold, sir," said his lordship, "the ghost is an excellent witness, and his evidence the best possible...but he cannot be heard by proxy in this court. Summon him hither, and I'll hear him in person, but your communication is mere hearsay, which my office compels me to reject."

Of course some of these stories are pretty convincing. Even his lordship might have accepted a story they tell in Boiestown, on the Miramichi River, New Brunswick, about an old lumber-camp caretaker who died in a most peculiar fashion. They found him on the lumber-camp floor surrounded by slices of plug tobacco, his pipe unfilled. He was a great pipe-smoker and since his death, his ghost has often been seen by lumbermen. They say he sits there on his grave, holding out an empty pipe as if he'd just love to have a smoke. Someone once tossed a plug of tobacco toward the grave...and next day it was gone. So from then on, it became the custom to provide this pipe-smoking ghost with his plug of MacDonald's Virginia Leaf.

Still in New Brunswick, there is a place up the Nashwaak River called Nixon Hollow, between Tay Creek and Stanley Village, and here is how it got its name. One night, many years ago, a man by the name of Nixon was on his way from Fredericton carrying a sackful of money to pay a road-building crew. Some of the men who had been drinking waylaid Nixon and killed him. They not only killed him...they beheaded him, and then, overcome by what they'd done, they hastily gathered up the head and buried it in the woods. No one knows where, of course, so the ghost of this man Nixon keeps coming back to Nixon's Hollow...looking for his head. It would be no good to offer *him* anything to smoke—not until he's found his head anyway.

On Lancaster Avenue, in Saint John West, there is the ghost of an old lady who keeps appearing. She rocks back and forth in a rocking chair...and she, also, has no head. I am afraid I don't know how she lost hers.

If you should be in Albert County this Hallowe'en, crossing a covered bridge at Bennett Lake, don't be surprised if you should pass a headless man lurking in the shadows. They have several headless men in Albert County. Back across the Bay of Fundy, in Annapolis Royal, it is an arm that is missing. The poor fellow lost it in a duel. It is just too bad we cannot help find replacements for all these missing parts.

However, whether it be mysterious wavering lights, glimmering white horses, or headless people, these are all well-behaved ghosts and part of the fun of Hallowe'en.

◆

FIRES OF UNKNOWN ORIGIN

If you are a member of a local fire department, you will know how frustrating it is, and how annoying, to be summoned to a false alarm. This past Hallowe'en a rash of these false alarms kept many fire departments up half the night. Fires were set as Hallowe'en pranks—something to create a big blaze and lots of smoke and get everybody all worked up. When the fire department gets there it is only a pile of old automobile tires, and a pall of smoke with the occasional flame jetting into the night sky. The fire engine brakes to a halt, sirens screaming, and the children who set the blaze watch from behind a hedge of spruce trees, hugging themselves with merriment. It is great fun getting the fire department out, seeing all these men rushing about with their fire helmets on, unravelling hoses and brandishing fire extinguishers. Everybody is excited. The whole neighbourhood is hurrying to see what's happening. All this activity because of a few old automobile tires, and you get these results just by lighting a match. It is better than television any day. Well, there is no real harm done. Nothing gets burnt up, at least nothing of any value.

It is simply that it is annoying to the fire department to have to answer a false alarm. And then too it just might keep them from answering a more serious alarm.

"a false alarm...just might keep the fire departments from answering a more serious alarm."

Also, there is always the possibility that that harmless little grass fire, set by the boys to get the fire department going, can get out of hand. It did in September of 1921, when a fire destroyed a good part of historic Annapolis Royal, N.S. This was the work of a youngster who thought he would touch a match to some straw in a stable so he could watch the fire engines working. It had been a long dry summer, that summer of 1921, and soon the fire department found itself without any water.... One third of the town burned down.

So sometimes even these little pranks can turn into tragedies, something the children didn't mean to cause and had not the slightest intention of causing. When it happens, it is too late.

Now you would think every effort would be made to teach children that fires are dangerous and that on no account—no possible account—should a building be set on fire. We *do* teach them this. We lecture them religiously on the dangers of fire. Schools have special speakers in to warn the children about these things—often a member of the local fire department. I am sure we all support the local fire department in conducting this anti-fire crusade.

But then look what happens. This same fire department will go out and set fire to some old abandoned building and stand around and watch it burn down. Instead of demolishing old buildings it is felt to be much faster and cheaper to burn them down. Maybe it is, but there is one thing the authorities are forgetting. Watching those fires are the children of the neighbourhood, because there is nothing that excites and draws children like seeing a building on fire.

Here are the grown men of their community, giving them such a wonderful example... the members of the fire department, running about with buckets of gasoline and kerosene oil, getting the blaze going, standing back and making sure everything is well on fire, with plenty of good draft. There's a window up there needs to be smashed in, well throw a rock up at it. The kids are taking it all in. Oh yes, they are watching everything and tucking away this information for future reference. Next time, why stop at some old used automobile tires? Burning down houses is much more fun.

Look at some of the fun the children have been having now they know how to do it.

This past February (1971), on Valentine's Day, the day dedicated to love, Christ Church, a 200-year-old church in Shelburne, N.S., was burned to the ground. Nothing in the church was saved. Several priceless relics went up in the blaze, including the paten and chalice which were a gift from Sir William Pepperell. Origin of the blaze—unknown.

Here is one where the origin of the blaze *was* known. A bridge over the Miramichi River, at Red Bank, N.B., was set afire by a group of children just about a year ago, last fall. This was a big highway bridge. Its replacement is going to cost one and a half million dollars. That was a honey of a blaze. It was so good, in fact, that another bridge over the Miramichi, not far from this bridge at Red Bank, was set on fire and destroyed this past summer, on July 3. That was just some high jinks saved over from Dominion Day.

Still in New Brunswick, in September, an old barn burned down in the vicinity of Woodstock, which would hardly have excited comment, except that in the ruins were found the bodies of two people later identified as two young men from Woodstock. And no one knows how that fire started.

On October 13, in the town of Chatham, an unoccupied two storey dwelling, just off Wellington Street, was completely levelled by fire. According to the *Miramichi Press*, this same house had suffered slight damage from a fire which broke out several weeks earlier. At that time, the blaze had been discovered and quickly extinguished. This last time the pranksters returned with a really good supply of gasoline.

Now I see in this week's Hartland *Observer* that fire of an unknown origin demolished a barn at Knowlesville. In this blaze only a few pigs lost their lives.

And so it goes...on and on...fires of unknown origin. All these children are doing is simply following the example of their local fire department. When they see *them* setting fires and burning down buildings, deliberately, can you blame the kids for taking a leaf from their book and having a little fun on their own?

◆

Religious Intolerance and Guy Fawkes Day

NO PIGS ALLOWED

"...he did not approve of...pigs. What this had to do with religion escapes me."

There once lived an outstanding leader on Prince Edward Island called Duncan McDonald. He was a minister of the Church of Scotland. The Rev. Duncan McDonald had uncanny powers of persuasion. According to an eyewitness who once heard him preach, "He would begin his sermons in a low, conversational tone, then, as he went on, his voice would become stronger, his delivery more urgent, and the whole man would preach—countenance, eyes, feet, hands, body—all would grow eloquent" as his listeners sat mesmerized, hungry for his words.

With spell-binding charisma, the Rev. Duncan McDonald ruled in patriarchal fashion over his several thousand followers. What he said was law. Two things he did not approve of were cradles and pigs.

What this had to do with religion escapes me. It seems to have been simply a personal idiosyncrasy. The Rev. Duncan McDonald just did not like the idea of putting babies in cradles, or of anyone keeping pigs. He went so far as to discourage his followers from having anything to do with pigs and, according to a farm census taken during his lifetime, the pig population on P.E.I. declined by over 2,000 head.

What minister do we have among us today, who could make the pig population go down by even so much as a hundred!

What minister have we who could make his flock toe the line, the way a Baptist minister once did at Chance Harbour, New Brunswick. According to a history of Chance Harbour, written in diverting style by Ethel Thompson, right in the middle of a sermon, a woman took exception to something the preacher said. She got up and walked out of church. Well, next Sunday, another parishioner, who lived next door to the church, happened to remember she'd left a pot of potatoes cooking on the stove. They were sure to burn before the service was over, so she decided to slip out, remove the pot and return to church. But the moment she stood up, the minister pointed a finger at her and said, "Sit down, Sister." She sat...and the potatoes burned.

This delicious sense of being able to order others around sometimes spilled over into the congregation itself, who found it extremely attractive to let their neighbours know how their lives might be improved. In 1880, five members of the Chance Harbour Baptist Church found themselves on a committee to hear complaints brought against other members of the congregation. Among the charges were drinking alcoholic beverages, dancing, and card playing. As a result of these charges, many members were either dropped or excluded from fellowship.

Point du Chene, near Shediac, N.B., is a favourite seaside resort. Among the original settlers of Point du Chene were the Simpson family and the MacDonald family. One went to the Church of England, the other was Roman Catholic. Now it happened that a MacDonald fell in love with Jane Simpson, but Jane Simpson's father objected to the marriage because MacDonald was not Church of England. Like Romeo and Juliet, the star-cross'd lovers almost didn't make it to the altar. Then the rector of the Anglican church came forward, the Rev. George S. Jarvis of St. Martin-in-the-Wood Anglican Church, and offered to perform the marriage ceremony—which he did. Upon this, the bride's father came forward and threatened to horsewhip Mr. Jarvis for having married his daughter to a Catholic. Whether he actually carried out the threat is uncertain. The case did get far enough to be recorded in legal documents as an action for assault.

Sectarian outbursts of this sort have been mercifully infrequent in this part of Canada where we might have expected the religious quarrels of Scotland to have been imported, along with the bagpipes. In fact, most of the quarrels were among the Presbyterians of Pictou County, N.S. Between Protestant and Catholic, there has always been friendly co-operation, in Pictou, Antigonish, and Cape Breton, through such events as the Highland Games and the activities of the Burns and St. Andrew's Societies.

Even mid-Victorian Halifax could muster very little public support for the celebrating of the anti-Catholic Guy Fawkes Day, on November 5, with its traditional goose supper. True, they had a bonfire on the Grand Parade on the evening of every November 5, when the Pope was usually burnt in effigy, but it signified very little. This was not England, or Ireland, but Nova Scotia, which, in 1822, had removed the impediments against Roman Catholics holding office—the first of Britain's North American colonies to do so.

Shortly after 1857, November 5 passed with no bonfire being kindled on Halifax's Grand Parade—and there's never been one since. Guy Fawkes Day just didn't catch on.

◆

"FOR THOSE IN PERIL ON THE SEA"

First Settler's Cemetery, Broad Cove, N.S.

Last fall, while visiting Broad Cove in Lunenburg County, I discovered in the middle of the village a very neat and well-tended cemetery called the First Settlers' Cemetery. And inside the gates, as I wandered among the stones, I came on this inscription:

In memory of Joseph, son of Joseph and Mary Smith, who fell from the main boom of the schn. J.B. Huey off White Head and was drowned Jan. 24, 1865. Aged 22 years.

Here, in these few poignant words was called up, starkly, the rigours and challenge of the great days of the sailing ships—the age when hymns like "Let Your Lower Lights be Burning" had a very special meaning for the people along our fog-shrouded coast...and that other old hymn that ended with the words, "Oh, hear us when we cry to Thee, for those in peril on the sea!"

Since visiting that First Settlers' Cemetery it has been brought home to me that these sea tragedies are still very much with us, and that the simple little headstone in Broad Cove is only one of many such monuments you will find throughout the country.

In this sombre month of November, forever associated with thoughts of remembrance, let us see how others, in other parts of the Maritimes, have paid tribute to those who were "in peril on the sea."

First, of course, one thinks of a lofty monument at the entrance to Halifax Harbour, a memorial to those in the services who lost their lives at sea in the two World Wars. This granite Cross of Sacrifice commemorates the more than 3,000 Canadian and Newfoundland naval and merchant sailors who were lost at sea. It is appropriate that the monument should be here on the shores of Point Pleasant Park, close by the main channel through which the ships pass, entering and leaving the harbour. Many of these men sailed past this very spot perhaps on their first and last voyage.

But in those grim years of World War II, Halifax was not the only east coast Canadian port. The dockside at Saint John, N.B., echoed to the sound of swinging derricks and puffing donkey engines, and in Courtenay Bay the dry dock worked around the clock repairing wartime casualties. If you should find yourself in East Saint John, in the vicinity of Courtenay Bay, take time out to look for a monument that faces the dry dock. On it is recalled one of the war's most heroic sea battles. It says,

Memorial Bell, Digby, N.S.

In Honoured Memory of Captain E. S. Fogarty Fegen, V.C., Officers and Men of H.M.S. Jervis Bay, who gave their lives in a gallant action against overwhelming odds with a German raider in the North Atlantic, November 5, 1940, in order that 38 ships under her care might be saved.

Captain Fogarty Fegen had sailed in and out of Saint John a good many times before that last trip. He and the crew of the *Jervis Bay* had made many loyal friends in the city, and for years after the war, church services were held to honour their memory.

There are, in fact, church services held in several coastal communities for the *fishermen,* to honour those who have not returned

home. In Lunenburg, N.S., in a very moving ceremony at the wharfside, wreaths of flowers are thrown upon the outgoing tide. In the Fishermen's Memorial Room in the town's Community Centre are listed the names of Lunenburg sailors who have lost their lives at sea.

In Digby, N.S., a Fishermen's Service is held on the town's Natal Day. The ceremony takes place at what is known as the Memorial Bell on Water Street. A ship's bell, standing as a symbol for Digby's salty way of life, surmounts this monument which carries the names of fishermen lost at sea out of Digby and the islands at the end of Digby Neck.

Just above the harbour at Escuminac, on New Brunswick's North Shore, stand the sculptured figures of three fishermen to mark the most tragic sea disaster in New Brunswick's history. On June 19, 1959, the waters of Miramichi Bay claimed the lives of 35 fishermen, victims of a freak hurricane that lashed the Bay with winds of up to 70 miles an hour.

The monument at Escuminac, the three fishermen standing with their heads shrouded with their oilskin hoods, is the work of sculptor Claude Roussel. It contains not only the names of the 35 fishermen; on a second bronze tablet are recorded the names of sixteen men who were recognized for acts of bravery in saving the lives of others. Two men, Bernard Jenkins, and his nephew Cyril Jenkins, each received the British Empire Medal for his bravery during this storm.

This disaster at Miramichi Bay left women who were now widows, or mothers who had been dependent on single boys who had lost their lives. It left 83 fatherless children. A New Brunswick Fishermen's Disaster Fund was set up and the response was magnificent. The Queen and Prince Philip broke with tradition by contributing personally, and eventually $440,000 was raised to provide assistance to the survivors.

So, we do remember. These things have brushed very close to all of us. We understand what the monuments mean—even that simple little headstone at Broad Cove.

◆

Fisherman's Monument by William de Garthe, Peggys Cove, N.S.

THE MEN IN OILSKINS

Some years ago there appeared in the pages of the *Observer*, a weekly newspaper published in Hartland, New Brunswick, a photograph of a young man in a private's uniform of the First World War, with this explanation:

The above photo of Carleton County's first military death in World War One was found on a postcard which was apparently sold to raise money for war purposes, whether by the Legion or by the Women's Institute, is not known. Enquiries have elicited little information as to living relatives or where they reside. Anyone having information about this Carleton County native is asked to write to The Observer in Hartland. Our war dead should not be allowed to drop into oblivion.

Underneath this young man's photograph, which is a reproduction of the postcard, are printed these words: "Ptd. Wendell H. Holmes, Princess Patricia's Canadian Light Infantry. First Carleton County boy to die in defence of his country." Yet, by 1971, Ptd. Wendell H. Holmes was so little remembered that no one was really quite sure where he had lived in Carleton County.

I mention this because we rather flatter ourselves that we do remember these things. On too many occasions, however, it appears that we somehow manage to forget.

We quite easily forget those who risked their lives every time they ventured out to sea, whether as merchant seamen or as Grand Banks fishermen, or even in-shore fishermen—for submarines were sinking vessels within sight of the Nova Scotia and New Brunswick coast as far back as 1917.

In August of 1918 a German submarine surfaced in the Bay of Fundy, just south of Grand Manan. Through their periscope they had sighted a four-masted schooner, the *Dorfontein*, built in Saint John and on her maiden voyage to South Africa with a load of lumber. The commander of the U-boat ordered the crew off the ship and kept them as prisoners aboard his submarine for five hours, while the schooner was set afire. They were then allowed to escape in a lifeboat, and made their way to Gannet Rock Lighthouse.

Evelyn M. Richardson, in her delightful book, *My Other Islands*, tells how some of the fishermen off western Nova Scotia reacted to the idea of abandoning a ship they may have helped build with their own hands. Captain Clayton Morrissey, for example, who earned the title among the Grand Banks fleet as "the greatest fisherman of them all." Captain Morrissey stood six foot seven and took a size

15 shoe. His towering figure may be seen today in Gloucester, Mass., for it was Captain Morrissey who posed for the Gloucester Fishermen's Memorial monument, peering into the fog, his powerful hands on the sculptured wheel.

One day, in the spring of 1918, a German submarine surfaced near Captain Morrissey's fishing schooner and commanded it to heave to. The helmsman was about to do as the U-boat commander had ordered when Captain Morrissey jumped forward, seized the wheel, spun it around, and, within seconds, his vessel was bearing down on the sub head-on. It is the only case I've ever heard of where a fishing schooner undertook to ram a submarine. The submarine managed to submerge before being hit, and its captain decided to leave this fighting skipper in charge of the field, and go hunting for a more accommodating victim.

The big push in unrestricted submarine warfare had begun the year before. In that spring, the spring of 1917, a little schooner named the *Nelson A.*, out of Yarmouth, N.S., with a crew of 16, had been fishing on the La Have Banks and was on her way home, holds filled to the hatches with halibut and codfish. Her owner, as well as skipper, was Captain John Sims.

On this Sunday morning he was out on deck oiling his oilskins when a German submarine loomed up out of the fog, crossed their stern, and demanded to know what cargo they had aboard. Upon learning that they carried a hold full of fish the U-boat commander ordered them to load a dory with 500 pounds of halibut and all the butter in the lazaret, and bring it over to the submarine. Then he said to Captain Sims, "Now, get in the dories and start rowing."

When Captain Sims looked back at his ship, the thing he minded losing most was the sails. She had just been fitted out with a brand new suit of sails, and they looked so clean and white, standing up in the fog.

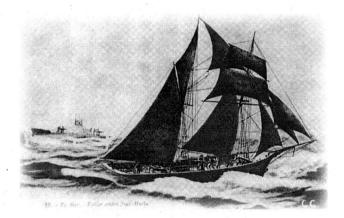

"...a German submarine loomed up out of the fog..."

On the deck happened to be two half-barrels, or half hogsheads, of fish oil. When the torpedo struck, it lifted these hogsheads high up off the deck and the fish oil splattered across the sails in a disfiguring scar. That seemed to hurt Captain Sims more than anything—seeing his new white sails, defiled by gurry and fish oil—that and the final glimpse of his vessel going under. "The last I saw of her," he told me, "was the end of her bowsprit going down."

They found themselves on Roseway Bank, 25 miles from land. They went ashore at Lockport, N.S. At the railway station the stationmaster would not let them on the train because they had no money. Their wallets had gone down with the ship, along with their good suits of clothes. But when the train pulled in, a friend who was on board saw that their fares were paid back to Yarmouth.

In one sense, these stories had a happy ending; there was no loss of life and no casualties. But there were fishermen, in both world wars, who were not so fortunate.

At this season of remembrance, let's not forget those other sailors whose uniform was a suit of oilskins.

◆

"We quite easily forget those who risked their lives every time they ventured out to sea..."

HOW DEER HUNTING
GOT STARTED IN NOVA SCOTIA

One summer morning I looked out of my bedroom window and here in the garden, browsing among the peas, were two deer—a buck and a doe—on their way down to the salt marshes. Princely animals, these. The buck gives an imperious toss of his head and disappears over the lilac hedge. The doe nibbles one final pea pod and then, suddenly, she is gone. It is a sight you'll not soon forget.

We did not always have these animals here in Nova Scotia. The deer you see in Nova Scotia today are recent introductions. They were brought in at the turn of the century, round about 1900.

The original deer of Nova Scotia became extinct some 400 years ago, and all because the Mi'kmaq were such famous hunters with their deadly bows and arrows. They also knew how to snare these animals, using an overhead snare made of twisted branches of the white birch. Sometimes they made a trap known as the dead fall, to release a great weight which fell on the animal and killed it.

A thousand years ago, the woods in Nova Scotia were full of deer. Then, about the year 1150, the North Atlantic suffered a serious worsening of the climate. The Arctic Current became filled with ice. Winter storms lasted longer and the snow gathered in great drifts. This made it easier for the Mi'kmaq to hunt the deer, herded together in "yards" for protection from the snow.

However they did it, the Mi'kmaq managed to make things very difficult for the deer until finally there were no deer left. By the time the first French settlers arrived, in the early 1600s, the deer in Nova Scotia were extinct, and no effort was made to replace the herds until the year 1901.

Among the pioneers who brought deer into the province was a young man who lived in Canning in the Annapolis Valley. Mr. Bishop travelled over to Saint John and obtained a pair of the native New Brunswick deer, from the curator of Rockwood Park. These were crated and shipped over to Digby by boat, then transported by train down the Annapolis Valley to Canning.

A corral made of wire, ten feet high, was constructed, half an acre of apple orchard was fenced off, and the deer became a great local attraction. It was worth driving all the way over from Pereau, or even from Wolfville, just to take a look. The blight of sophistication had not yet robbed the world of its early morning sense of wonder. People came in surreys, and market wagons, jogging over the sandy roads, across the dykes to Canning to see what a deer looked like. It was a grand outing for a Sunday, a picnic expedition. The girls enjoyed feeding leaves to the little faun that had just been born.

Well, it was great fun, but the deer needed constant attention, if they were to be kept out of trouble. One day the buck, in a prancing fit of high spirits, stepped on the little faun and broke its leg. The leg had to be tended to, a splint made. There were other problems; the deer started browsing among the apple trees, defoliated the lower branches. On one occasion they broke through the wire fence. They had become a chore.

So Mr. Bishop sold the three of them to a sporting lodge on the outskirts of Halifax—the Micmac Game and Fish Club. This was a few miles out on the St. Margaret's Bay Road, where the gentlemen of the city, in their Norfolk jackets, foregathered for a spot of grouse hunting, a fowling piece under one arm and a lady friend on the other.

Here the animals were allowed to run free. They seemed tame enough and quite contented. They hung about the lodge, waiting to be fed little delicacies, or given a pinch of salt. They became pets. And then one day, they were gone—leaving the gentlemen of the

"The gentlemen...plunged into the woods for a spot of hunting."

Game and Fish Club in something of a quandary.

By this time they (and their lady friends) had grown very fond of those deer. It was not nice to think of the poor animals, off there wandering alone through the woods where they might meet a Mi'kmaq with a bow and arrow, or even just a man from Halifax with one of the new lever-action carbines.

The gentlemen of the Game and Fish Club thought long and hard and then, with a sigh, they reached for their own carbines and plunged into the woods for a spot of hunting.

This is how all this deer hunting in Nova Scotia got started. The truth is, the gentlemen were very poor shots and they did not manage to put the deer out of their misery. The deer got away—at least, some of them.

In spite of the latest thing in telescopic sights, and bone-handled sheath knives, and beam-point flash lights, and a gleaming white deep freeze back home in the kitchen, the deer still keep getting away.

You know, the Mi'kmaq really knew how to hunt. *They* didn't let any get away. Maybe we'd better go back to bows and arrows for a change.

◆

ADVICE FROM AN OLD GUIDE

"We know that hunting is going to continue..."

We pulled into the roadside canteen and here was a car already parked. Hunters—the two men were inside the canteen, sitting up at the counter warming up on coffee and crullers. One had on a hunting jacket with a knitted neckband and a cloth-lined hood, high leather boots, a wide leather belt supporting a bone-handled sheath knife. The other was wearing a mackinaw which was open, exposing one of those reversible two-colour vests. One of his socks was rolled up to his knee; the other tucked down over the high leather boot.

In the warmth of the canteen, beads of sweat were beginning to stipple their brows. They were puffy men, with ruddy cheeks and good-natured lines around their eyes. One of them was venturing to engage the waitress in some gentle kidding, but the barbs were almost apologetic. These were faces that belonged behind a desk, or the teller's wicket. But now they were no longer office personnel. For the next three days they would be hunters. They were free men, free from their jobs, free from their wives, free to roam the woods, and wrest a living from Nature with nothing but their two bare hands, a gun, some insect repellent, a primus stove, a 20-piece aluminum nested cooking set, a full back packsack, and a soap holder, with cover.

Already it was beginning to tell on them because it isn't easy for a city man to throw off the shackles of civilization and revert to the primeval.

In the first place, he doesn't know how to dress. He fancies it's going to be cold out there in the woods, away off from everything, no doctors handy, no chance to use his Medicare card if he should come down with a cold. He'd better dress up good and warm.

The result is calamitous. After half an hour out from camp, he is beginning to pant. He has to sit down on the nearest log and take a swig from his thermos bottle—all because he doesn't know how to dress. Let us see if we can help make this hunting trip pleasanter.

Now some of you may object to this and say, "Why help people to hunt down these poor defenceless animals? Let them find out for themselves." Many people today, both in the city and out in the country, find the very thought of hunting distasteful. They dread the onset of the hunting season, and the annual parade of cars bearing the carcass of a deer—often a very small one—draped over the hood, or dangling from the roof.

As Canadians, we should remind ourselves that hunting is not a right, or a privilege, available to the citizen in every country. There's no such thing as hunting in Great Britain for the common man. In Europe there's not this mass exodus into the woods every fall. There are not the woods; there are not the animals.

In Canada, we still cling to a pioneer tradition that it is the right, or even the duty, of every able-bodied man to go prowling through the woods every fall in search of game with which to feed his hungry family. Now most of the families in Canada today, even with the spiralling grocery bill, are not that hungry. But we still go on hunting.

There is a reason we go on hunting that has nothing to do with food and, in a sense, nothing to do with hunting. For most hunters this is their one opportunity to get away by themselves, to escape from the maddening crowd and find themselves out there in the woods... alone...with a cushion of pine needles underfoot and, all around them, like a great encompassing blanket, the sounds, the smells, the colour and healing solace of the forest.

Let's be realistic. We know that hunting is going to continue; that this fall there will be more hunters in the woods than ever before; that we'll have the usual tally of accidents, and deaths, caused by too many hunters who don't know how to hunt, who wound but don't kill so that the animal is left to wander through the woods and, after days of lingering pain, creep away into some little valley to die.

"...we cling to a... tradition that it is... right...to go prowling through the woods every fall in search of game..."

I have just been talking to a neighbour of mine—a real hunter who for many years was a guide in the Nova Scotia woods, around Stillwater and Ponhook Lake. The real hunter knows how to get very close to his prey. He shoots to kill, not merely to wound. Here, then, are his tips on how to get that deer.

One of the main secrets of a real hunter is that he hunts only on days when it's raining—not a heavy pelting rain but a drizzling rain. On fine days, your scent carries; it travels with the wind. In fine weather, with a breeze blowing, a deer can smell you half a mile off. But when it's raining, your scent is carried down into the ground along with the rain. On a rainy day you might almost stumble over a deer before he'd see you because a deer's sight is not as good as a man's.

There is another reason why you should choose a rainy day. The rain makes a good deal of noise in the woods; it muffles your footsteps. You might come on a deer suddenly, and almost be able to reach out and touch him before he knows you are there—as long as it's raining. So forget about those crisp, bright autumn days; the time to go hunting is on a drizzly, rainy day.

You are going to get wet. But, oddly enough, you won't catch a cold so long as you keep moving. That is the important thing—to keep moving. The cold rain is uncomfortable at first, and then gradually your body adjusts to it and,

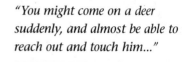

"You might come on a deer suddenly, and almost be able to reach out and touch him..."

if the rain stops, you may even arrive back at camp with dry clothes. Your clothes may dry on your body without your even being aware of it.

In order to keep moving, you must carry as little as possible. A jack-knife, with a blade that locks, is about all you need and your gun, of course, which has a safety catch. You make sure the safety catch is on at all times, until you are ready to shoot.

As to clothes, wear the lightest footgear you can buy—moccasins, even tennis shoes, if you can find a pair with extra thick soles. Do not wear heavy home-knit socks. Buy some light socks at the store and carry an extra pair to change into when the pair you have on become too soggy.

Wear your regular undershirt, not the heavy woollens, and a good substantial shirt over that. Over that again, a light wool sweater, a cardigan. Some wear a turtle-necked sweater, but you'll find that the turtle-necked sweater presses continually on your windpipe as you hike through the woods. A cardigan with a V neck is the more suitable. You will need a light cap—a red cap, of course.

This is the way you should dress in, let's say, November, on a day when it's snowing, as well as raining. First of all, make up your mind you are going to get wet. The first half mile your knees get wet, from the water dripping off the bushes. Then it starts to trickle down the back of your neck, and before long, you're wet all over. Once you get used to it you don't mind as long as you keep moving.

For food, carry a wedge of cheese and a lump of old-fashioned brown sugar—the kind that used to form lumps as hard as stone. These two items will sustain life and keep you from feeling hungry.

If you must have a hot drink, slip a tin can into your pocket and a handful of tea, with some matches in a water-tight pill bottle.

If you are looking for fuel to build a fire, you can always find tinder in the woods. At the base of most spruce trees you'll see little dead branches, the size of a knitting needle. They are always dry; they will always burn. Break off a bundle of these and crack up the smallest of them, some no bigger than a darning needle, until you have a little pile that will ignite. Then add the bigger branches and build it up until you have a camp fire. If it's a regular downpour, get in the lea of something, like an overhanging rock.

So, that is the old hunter's advice and now you've had your tea. You're wet all over, and you will have the satisfaction—if you enjoy that kind of thing, but many of us don't— of knowing you are about to get a deer.

And you're going to kill it. Not maim it.

◆

HOCKEY IN THE MARITIMES

The game of hockey is unique to Canada. It is our game. We made the rules and we play it supremely well. On Saturday night, from coast to coast, we can think of nothing else. If there is one thing that draws Canadians together and makes us into a team, it's hockey.

Like so many other things in this nation of ours, hockey was born right here in the Maritimes. We invented it. It got its start in Halifax and evolved gradually from a game called hurley, which in its early stages was a little bit like cricket. The reason it was like cricket is easy to see. Halifax, around about 1800, garrisoned hundreds of British troops whose officers were all accomplished cricketers...but not very good skaters.

The glistening expanse of Dartmouth Lakes and the North West Arm was something new to them. It was a real novelty and they decided to have some fun on it. So this game was devised. Hurley was a sort of attempt to play cricket on the ice, sometimes with the players wearing skates, but often simply sliding about on the ice as best they could, at times losing their balance and their dignity. They were like Mr. Pickwick, Mr. Wardle and Sam Weller at Dingley Dell. No doubt there were many tumbles during the game, and much good-natured laughter.

A newspaper report of 1805 describes a game between the Halifax Artillery Company and the Light Infantry which lasted "for upward of 6 hours, and ended in a draw game. Afterwards," the paper says, "both companies dined together, and ended the day in the utmost harmony and good humour."

Now this, I feel, is the true origin and appeal of hockey. It was a thing of conviviality, of good fellowship, socializing. The same spirit can be found among most hockey fans and players even today—in spite of those who throw pop bottles

Boys playing hockey outdoors in Windsor, N.S.

or enter into brawls and otherwise do their best to give the game a bad name. It did not start out that way. The fights and bloody noses came much later.

Until 1872, the game was played with a round ball. Then a Halifax goal-keeper introduced the rubber puck. Hockey sticks, or hurleys, as they were called, were bought from the Indians at the city's outdoors Green Market.

In 1875, the first game of true ice hockey was played in Montreal, under rules which had been drawn up by J. G. A. Creighton, who had merely imported the game to Montreal as he had seen it played in his home town of Halifax.

Halifax further refined the game, in 1899, with the introduction of the first goal nets. Till then there had been merely goal posts.

By this time, keen competition had developed between Maritime cities and towns, with Moncton, N.B., producing several teams of distinction such as the Moncton Mohawks and the Victorias who won five Maritime titles and two New Brunswick championships.

During the 1920s, Moncton developed a team that has remained unique in the history of Canadian hockey. Each member of the team was a son of John Carroll. During the

"... J.G.A. Creighton, who ... imported the game to Montreal... from Halifax."

1920s, this team, the Carroll Family Hockey Team, won many titles and trophies.

But already violence and disorder were beginning to show up on hockey night. At one game in Moncton against a team from Fredericton, a fight broke out between the players and several of them began swinging their sticks. A week later, when the Moncton team went to Fredericton to play, the police arrested one of these Moncton players, for his part in the fight at Moncton. With this the Moncton team left the rink and a riot broke out which ended with the fans chasing the referee around town.

These teams were of national stature. In 1933, the Allan Cup was won by the Halifax Wolverines. The same trophy was won the next year by the Moncton Hawks who defeated Fort William, Hamilton, and McGill University.

In all this competitiveness, let's not lose sight of the friendly side of the game which still remains—getting out to the game, meeting friends and neighbours, and admiring the

"... George Warden... elected to the Nova Scotia Sports Hall of Fame..."

spectacle of speed and physical prowess.

This friendly side of hockey was brought home to me a few years ago, while I was travelling back and forth between Halifax and Hantsport on the Dominion Atlantic Railway. The conductor on this run was a most courteous man, thoughtful, ready to lend a hand. Often I would get off the train and leave things up on the luggage rack—a camera, some books. He would see them and next day our agent would phone to say my camera or books were waiting at the station.

Not once did the conductor, George Warden, mention to me that he had been elected to the Nova Scotia Sports Hall of Fame and voted Sportsman of the Year for 1964. Only after his death did I read in the paper the outstanding contributions this man had made to sport—hockey in particular.

As a star defenceman, he had played with the Kentville Wildcats, and Berwick Apple Kings, and later with the Truro Junior Bearcats. After his own active days of playing were over, he, with his brother Albert and a friend, Arthur Lightfoot, founded Canada's

first hockey school in Kentville, N.S.—a school which became the model for similar hockey schools throughout Canada.

George Warden, in the many times I met him on the train, never mentioned a word of this. He was too busy watching out for absent-minded people, to make sure they didn't forget their baggage. When he wasn't working, he was helping youngsters to learn to play hockey and how to protect themselves from injury.

George Warden was a friendly man and I like to think he epitomized the best in Canadian hockey. Let's hope that in these international games, which have grown so popular, the George Wardens will prevail and that we will see fewer bloody noses, and a little more of the convivial spirit of Mr. Pickwick and Dingley Dell.

◆

Hockey sweaters of the "Shamrocks"– Champions of the Kings County Junior League in 1906, 1907 and 1908.

HOW TO AVOID FREEZING
IN THE DARK

"... when they used Aladdin gas lamps to read by..."

Do you remember away back, when your family first moved to Saint John from up the Belleisle? Or to Halifax from Rose Bay or Clam Harbour? What a time that was! A whole wide spectrum of new and exciting sights, scenes and activities was spread out before you—tennis courts, concerts, public libraries, night classes.

Opportunities beckoned from every side. For awhile, you exploited these advantages to the utmost. That was a long time ago, wasn't it? Now the magic has gone and everything is taken for granted. Familiarity breeds, if not contempt, some complacency.

It is the same with new inventions. Think of the coming of electricity, for example. The people of Woodstock, New Brunswick no longer treat electricity as the magical thing it is, because they've grown so accustomed to it. You see, they've had electricity in Woodstock for almost 90 years. So at this point it is kind of silly getting excited about the dishwasher, or wondering if perhaps you are not using it thriftily. Electricity has been lighting the streets of Woodstock for as long as anyone can remember. Everyone expects it to go on being there like tomorrow's dawn. Suppose you did forget to turn the light off over the front door, don't worry. It is not that important, not like it was 90 years ago, when the people who lived in Woodstock felt it a privilege to turn on that first switch. Most of them are gone now. No one in Woodstock remembers what it was like when electricity first came to town.

This is something of a pity because, in this time of soaring energy costs, those of us who've always enjoyed this convenience without giving it a thought may be in for some chilly reminders. It leaves us terribly vulnerable and suggestible to those who would have us believe we are going to "freeze in the dark." We stand like bewildered children shuddering at these scare headlines, so let me reassure you.

In the district of Clinton, Prince Edward Island, no one was "freezing in the dark" back thirty years ago. The people of Clinton were very comfortable, in fact. Yet, it was not until several years later, until the fall of 1954, that a power line reached the district of Clinton and other communities on the Island. Lots of folks living on the Island today can remember what it was like when they used Aladdin gas lamps to read by and wood-burning stoves to do the cooking.

"…and used wood-burning stoves to do the cooking."

It was the same in rural Lunenburg County where electrification came only after the Second World War, during the early fifties.

Other parts of the Maritimes, too, have not forgotten the thrill of having electricity, for the first time, take over a dozen household chores. It came to Pugwash in the early 1920s, to Grand Manan Island in the Christmas season of 1929. In the villages of Isaacs Harbour and Goldboro, in Guysborough County, the end of the oil lamp came in the summer of 1940.

I have visited households where electricity is still treated with the respect it deserves, and have picked up some pointers about how to keep that power bill to a minimum...without freezing in the dark. Here they are.

They do not waste energy heating rooms that are not used. A surprising number of home owners continue, all through the winter, to heat the spare bedroom when no one is using it. Why not close it off?

Some make a point of pulling all the shades and drapes before going to bed. Others turn off the thermostat and use an extra blanket, unless it promises to be a really frosty night.

In the kitchens of these energy efficient

homes I did not once see the electric or gas oven being used to heat the room or to prepare dishes that could just as well be done in an electric frying pan—which consumes only a tenth of the power.

Refrigerators, too, were being put to maximum service, and not being used to store things that don't belong there, like canned corn or canned asparagus. Some householders supplemented their refrigerator with a cool, but insulated back porch, where many food items could be kept during the winter—bottles of pop or vegetables like turnips.

These people always covered their utensils to bring them to the boil faster, and they used pots and pans of the right size for the element so that unused heat did not escape into the room.

Does this sound like too much bother? Well, if we thoughtlessly take our modern conveniences for granted, I suppose we may some day find ourselves—if not freezing in the dark—maybe toasting our toes in a wood-stove oven, under the glow of an Aladdin lamp.

◆

THE EVE OF ST. NICHOLAS

...he wears his bishop's robes. He carries an ecclesiastical staff."

Already the loud speakers on Main Street are playing "Silver Bells." Truck-loads of pine and spruce and fir are coming into town to be used for covering rose bushes and decorating the lattice-work on the front porch. Tonight, the firemen will be around selling boxes of chocolates in holly and mistletoe wrappings for the benefit of our local fire department. The kids will be at the window, watching for the big fire truck with its flashing red light. On the bulletin board at the post office, there is a notice from the Rebeccas reminding members to bring presents for the shut-in boxes and a contribution for children in hospital. We are starting to think about Christmas.

Already the kids are drafting those letters to Santa Claus but they will have to wait three more weeks—that is, unless they are lucky enough to be Dutch, in which case they will be able to enjoy *two* Christmas Eves: one on December 24, the other one on December 5, the eve of the Feast of St. Nicholas.

This is one of the genial customs which has been brought out to Canada by settlers from the Netherlands. I think most kids would like to see it catch on and become a regular Canadian institution.

Imagine, two Christmas Eves—two opportunities to hang up your stocking! If St. Nicholas does not bring that gyro spin car, or the electronic bowling game, perhaps by Christmastime Santa might be in a more solvent mood.

But first, a word about this fellow St. Nicholas. Most of us think of St. Nicholas as Santa's European *alter ego*. In fact, the name Santa Claus is simply a corruption of St. Nicholas. (It is the way St. Nicholas sounds when you say it in Dutch.)

Santa Claus, as I am sure everyone knows, sprang from the imagination of one man, Clement Clarke Moore, an American who wrote a set of verses called "A Visit from St. Nicholas." It begins with those famous words, "Twas the night before Christmas." From these verses has been drawn the popular conception of Santa Claus, fat, jolly, and entirely secular.

St. Nicholas is a very different character. He was, in fact, a real man—a bishop who lived during the fourth century in Asia

Minor. After his death, he became the patron saint of Russia and of children everywhere. When he comes to visit the children on December 5—as he does in every Dutch home—he wears his bishop's robes. He carries an eccles-iastical staff. He is, with his long white beard, a very dignified, a very impressive figure.

As with Santa Claus, the children come forward and sit on his knee and tell him of the gifts they are dreaming about. Then, later on, they place their shoes beside the chimney or alongside the stove and, in the morning, the shoes will be stuffed full of goodies.

Much of this I learned from a neighbour of mine who was born in Holland and came out to this country after the war as a bride. At that time, there was a wave of immigration from the Netherlands to the Annapolis Valley, beginning around about 1950, and continuing for the next 16 years or so. That is when most of these 70 or 80 families came out to the Annapolis Valley from the Netherlands. It was for many of them a big move—a daunting experience.

But it was done under a certain amount of official supervision. The man in charge of this was Allen B. Foley, of Kentville, whose job as placement and settlement officer with the Department of Immigration, brought him

"He is, with his long white beard, a very dignified...impressive figure."

in close contact with these families who were trying to adjust to Canadian ways, facing problems of language or financing the purchase of a farm. Mr. Foley, who came to take a personal interest in the settlement of these families, would pitch in and lend a hand with the haying or help in stumping a piece of new land.

He knew, perhaps as well as anyone, how much they had sacrificed to pay off the mortgages on their farms. Whatever they have gone in for—whether dairy farming, raising pigs, growing tobacco, they have carried it through successfully. This success depends upon one thing—hard work, for which they have a great capacity. These Dutch farmers are an industrious people.

Yet, despite this—or perhaps because of it—they are great hands for having parties. They like celebrations. One celebration they go in for is the 12 year wedding anniversary, which I found puzzling until it was pointed out to me that 12 years is half way to the silver wedding anniversary.

Some of the old customs are dying out. You do not too often see the traditional wooden shoes, though some of the older generation still wear them around the farm or garden and they tell me these Dutch wooden shoes, or *klompen*, as they are called, when properly made to fit the individual foot, can be very comfortable and are just the thing to set out beside the fireplace to hold those gifts from St. Nicholas.

Every year, on the eve of St. Nicholas Day, Netherlanders throughout the Annapolis Valley used to hold a big get-together at the Lion's Hall in Berwick. Some years, as many as 200 people turned up, and at the party St. Nicholas put in an appearance, along with his lively helper, Black Peter. Black Peter is a sort of court jester. He carries a big bag full of presents, but he also runs about switching people if they don't behave themselves. If they have been very bad—especially if they

"...wooden shoes...are just the thing to set out beside the fireplace... to hold those gifts from St. Nicholas."

are little boys and girls—there is always the chance he will pop them into his bag and take them back to his home in Spain.

At this rollicking affair, people from each province of the Netherlands had a chance to perform their local music. The master of ceremonies asked those from North Holland, or South Holland to step forward and they sang the song or anthem that identified their homeland. Then he asked the Canadians to step forward and sing "O Canada." Then there was dancing and musical chairs, and the refreshments which are always a memorable part of the evening when Dutch people get together.

So, think of those lucky kids who will be putting out their shoes on St. Nicholas Eve for the kindly saint to fill, and Santa Claus still to come! With that as a bonus, who wouldn't wear wooden shoes?

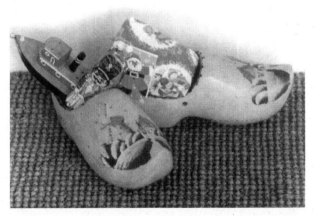

THREE CHILDREN
AND THE HALIFAX EXPLOSION

There is this life raft designed to hold four people but there are five of you. If anyone is to survive, one must be pushed off the raft to save the rest. That's the situation.

It is part of an exercise called Values Education, intended to get children thinking about moral values. Some critics say that by encouraging this sort of "do-it-yourself" morality we may end up with kids who wouldn't save a drowning man if they could think of a good reason not to. These sorts of dilemmas present questions that require decisions which are pretty difficult for children in Grades 7 or 8 but are no bigger than the real-life decisions that faced the children in Halifax's public schools, on the morning of December 6, 1917, when a ship carrying a fantastically large cargo of TNT blew up in the harbour. The situations faced by *those* children were just as grim as any presented in a decision-making exercise.

In the many accounts that have come down to us of this disaster there is no suggestion of people being pushed outside in order that someone else might survive. Quite the contrary, the Halifax Explosion has left us a record of men, women, and children thinking of others, not of themselves—sticking to their posts, trying to lend a hand, enduring

suffering and loss which we can only dimly guess at.

Among the children who witnessed this calamity, were three who would one day tell what they had seen on that awful morning—novelist Hugh MacLennan, novelist Evelyn M. Richardson, novelist and historian Thomas H. Raddall. Each one has given powerful and compelling testimony that the Haligonians of 1917 knew quite a lot about "values."

Hugh MacLennan embodied his memories of that day in his novel *Barometer Rising,* considered by many as the book that launched Canadian fiction. Much of its detail he had either seen himself or learned from his father, a doctor specializing in surgery, who spent the week following the explosion at the hospital. He was operating constantly and was a witness to the spirit of these people—so many cut and burned about the face, yet ready to give up their turn to someone in greater need.

The personal experience of Thomas H. Raddall, then a student at Chebucto Road School, provided the material for a sombre and vivid chapter in his absorbing autobiography *In My Time.*

Falling plaster had left the classroom at Chebucto School "filled with a fog of white dust." Some of the children had been cut with flying glass, but he says, "I don't recall much crying out. For a few seconds we stood like a lot of powdered clowns with badly applied daubs of red paint here and there." Then, "with the instinct born of routine fire-practice," they go to their cloak-rooms and "clatter away downstairs to run home." He reports no panic, no one jostling to get out first.

Richmond School, after the Halifax Explosion, 1917.

At the Halifax Academy, on Sackville Street opposite the Citadel, Evelyn M. Richardson was in the Assembly Hall on the third, or top, floor. Her recollections of that morning were published in The *Nova Scotia Historical Quarterly*. She says,

…most of us sat stunned and expecting a second blast. At the back of the Hall four girls rose and started for the stairs, where panic and tragedy could follow the least mishap on the old winding, plaster-and-glass buried steps. A quick-witted classmate sprang to the doorway and barred it with her outstretched arms; the four girls turned and quietly resumed their seats. In the meantime the history teacher had walked unhurriedly to the Fire Exit at the front of the Hall; now he stood beside the opened door as the principal, with controlled face and voice, dismissed us with, 'Rise and proceed as for Fire Drill'. Two by two, as in regular practices, the girls marched out and down the fire-escape.

Then she says,

…one account of that day mentions 'the panic that swept the city'…There must have been some early panic, though I saw only stunned endurance. There was also courage and fortitude. What else held the Academy boys 'at attention' by their chairs, white-faced but steady, like the sons and brothers of soldiers that they were, until the last girls had marched past them, and they could fall in line? Though they believed the city was being shelled and knew that another hit would flatten the racked Academy.

Of course, Evelyn Richardson and the other students at the Academy were among the lucky ones—though perhaps not so lucky by the time they had finally reached home and understood what had really happened.

At Richmond School, the building collapsed, killing a hundred students and many teachers. All the staff of the Protestant Orphanage died, along with 200 children and, at St. Joseph's Orphanage, 50 children died.

For them there wasn't even the chance to decide who would be allowed to survive.

◆

FOOTSTEPS IN THE SNOW

Most of us, if set down in the middle of the woods, would begin to worry about the likelihood of meeting a bear, or a wildcat, or some other fierce denizen of the forest—even a panther. Last winter, an eastern panther was seen near the St. Andrews municipal dump at Chamcook. The man who saw it described it as "about the size of a Labrador retriever, lank, glossy and jet-back…its shape and pattern of movement just like a great big cat."

It would be pretty scary to meet an eastern panther somewhere in the woods but the chances of his attacking you are not really that great. It is now thought that the eastern panther has been in New Brunswick for at least 50 years though seldom sighted. We know of no cases where it has attacked humans.

Generally speaking, such animals are as anxious to get out of your way as you are to avoid them. So it is a good idea to know *how* to avoid them, which really means how to read the signs and to be able to tell if they are in the vicinity.

"… they came on footsteps in the snow…what do you suppose it was?…"

Then, of course, there is always the chance you might encounter the tracks of one of those strange science-fiction creations, half-animal, half-man that have been puzzling the scientific world for many years. In California, they call it the Bigfoot. In the Himalayas, it is known as the Abominable Snowman. On our own west coast, in British Columbia, they have made plaster casts of footprints that were 17 inches long from heel to toe. Do we have anything like that here, lurking in the less frequented parts of New Brunswick or Nova Scotia?

On the Magdalen Islands, back about a hundred years ago, they came on footsteps in the snow that were 22 inches long and a foot wide. No bear has a footprint that big. What do you suppose it was?

Well, they finally caught up with this thing and luckily they did not kill it. The monster survived and here is its story.

In mid-December of 1872, a raging blizzard hit Grindstone Island and for several days people stuck close to their homes. When the wind began to let up, three boys decided to go down to the beach to see what driftwood had floated in. Here they found the wreckage of a ship, scattered up and down the shore.

The boys went among the wreckage, gathering salvage, and, after it grew dark, they lighted flares to see their way home. Suddenly, from out of the wreckage there appeared this monster—eight feet high and snow white. It approached them slowly, making what sounded like unfriendly sounds. The boys took to their heels and ran as fast as they could for home.

Breathlessly, they told what they'd seen, but no one paid any attention to their story. It was probably a polar bear that had drifted in.

Next day, some twenty men went down to the beach to gather salvage from the wreck. That night, on their way home, they passed a hay barn and, once again, this fantastic white figure loomed up from out of the snow and began to come slowly toward them. The men were terrified. They dropped everything and ran.

Once back in the village, they called at the home of their priest, Father Charles Boudreault, and told him of this ghostly apparition. He did not know what to make of such a story and tried to calm their fears. He told them that, in the morning, if they would meet him at the church, they would all return to the beach and investigate the matter.

Next day, when Father Boudreault appeared at the church, he found that very few of his congregation were there to meet him. Only about a dozen men showed up and each of them carried a gun. At first they found nothing. It seemed the creature had disappeared, perhaps returned to the sea. Or had they imagined it all?

All at once Father Boudreault gave a gasp of astonishment and hurried forward to examine something. There, in the snow, clearly moulded, were the outlines of immense footprints—almost two feet long. What could it be?

They finally caught up with this gigantic creature. It had fallen on the beach and lay there unable to get up. It was nine feet in girth and eight feet long. The head was almost three feet long and four feet wide with cavities where the eyes and mouth would be.

Father Boudreault leaned over to examine the head, and as he did so the creature uttered a cry. "Father!" it said, "Father!"

Father Boudreault then realized that this vast bulk consisted of ice and snow and that inside was a man who had recognizd his Roman collar and the silver cross he wore.

"Quick," he said. "He must be got back to the village. Fetch some planking from the wreck."

It took every last one of those dozen men to carry this huge block of ice back to the village, for it weighed over half a ton. When they had carefully chipped the ice away they found, underneath, a giant of a man—six feet eight inches in height and weighing 310 pounds.

Because of his immense size and tremendous physique, this man, Auguste Le Bourdais, the lone survivor of the shipwreck, had lived through hours in the icy water while clinging to a piece of floating wreckage. Later, on land, he had wandered about in the snow for days as the snow clung to him and gathered like a snowball, then turned into a block of ice.

Le Bourdais lost both legs from that ordeal. Later, after an operation in Quebec, he was fitted with peg legs and returned to the Magdalens where he lived the rest of his life. To this day, on the Magdalens, they will speak of it as the "miracle of Le Bourdais."

◆

*"In mid-December of 1872,
a raging blizzard hit..."*

CHRISTMAS CAROLS AND THE PIANO

The greens are all up now—wreaths of ground juniper and fir bedecked with gilded pine cones, or a string of coloured lights. Most of us have our lights, outlining a tree, a shrub, or a doorway. Once again, you hear the Christmas music from house radios and loudspeakers along Main Street... and even at the bank. For the past few weeks, faithful choir members have been practising for a special Christmas Eve carol service.

"... gather about the piano and sing... songs that celebrate the spirit of Christmas."

We take it all so much for granted. We're even a trifle bored and turn the music off. You hear people saying, "Do they have to play those records all the time? We'll be tired of them by Christmas. They should be outlawed for awhile!"

We don't really mean that, because if we did ban them we'd soon be meeting together secretly at friends and neighbours, to gather about the piano and sing these songs that celebrate the spirit of Christmas.

That is exactly what took place in Puritan times when Christmas carols *were* banned. It is funny how the Puritans—well-meaning people in so many ways—did not seem to realize what difficult ground they were on when they made Christmas celebrations illegal, including the singing of Christmas carols.

What happened was that Christmas went underground. Instead of the public revels and lord mayor's banquet, there began the modern approach to Christmas; a more private celebration, with families being reunited, friends getting together to raise their voices in song.

Almost a hundred years would pass before carol-singing returned to the churches, when Dr. Isaac Watts, a nonconformist minister, wrote and introduced to his congregation a carol that was the forerunner of the many carols you hear today. "Joy to the World" it was called.

Most of our carols are not really that old and a surprising number were written by Americans—"It Came Upon a Midnight Clear,"

"...one way...to pick up the latest tunes...was with a piano and ... printed music."

"We Three Kings of Orient Are," and one of the most popular of all, "O Little Town of Bethlehem," written in 1868, by Bishop Phillip Brookes of Boston.

It is easy enough today to learn the latest songs. All you have to do is listen to the records. A song like "Rudolph the Red-nosed Reindeer" rockets suddenly to fame right across the country. The first recording of that song, by Gene Autry, was released on September 19, 1949, and by October 15, in less than a month, it was a hit.

But how did people learn to sing Christmas songs before they had recordings or radios? There was just one way to do it. Somehow or other, you had to secure that new and exciting musical instrument, the piano. Later on, of course, you could buy a parlour organ; they became very popular. For those first families up the St. John River, or over in Summerside, there was only one way they could pick up the latest tunes and get the harmonies. That was by means of a piano

and some printed music. It is surprising how many pioneering families did manage to acquire a piano or one of those instruments that preceded the piano, like the spinet or harpsichord.

In the New Brunswick Museum in Saint John, among their collection of heritage furniture, is a most unusual instrument known as an Angelica which consists of 25 tuned glasses, covering two full octaves, housed in a rosewood cabinet, the whole thing supported by a massive circular base. This was brought out from England in 1836, by John Woodman of Saint John.

At Kings Landing, in the parlour of the Upper Farmhouse, is an instrument called the melodeon which was brought to New Brunswick in 1825—by ship, of course—from a firm from Boston.

About the same time, on Prince Edward Island, a Presbyterian minister arrived from Scotland and settled in the district of Belfast. He was the Rev. John MacLennan who was shortly to return to Scotland to fetch his bride-to-be. Mrs. MacLennan is still remembered in Belfast because of her vivacious and charming manner and also because she brought out from Scotland, along with her charm, her piano and the latest songs including some of these Christmas carols.

The people of P.E.I. must have been exceptionally fond of music for many pianos were brought to the Island during the nineteenth century. Robert Harris, the Island artist, whose painting "The Fathers of Confederation" is perhaps the best-known picture in Canada, enjoyed listening to his mother play Christmas carols on a piano that had been bought in Liverpool, England, in 1848.

Another instrument, brought to the Island in 1801, is a Clementi piano, a gift to Government House by Mr. and Mrs. Earl Baker. The P.E.I. Heritage Foundation recently had it shipped down to Boston to be restored, and it is now back in Government House.

Moving a piano, at the best of times, is no easy job. These people were without half-ton trucks, without railroads. In many cases there were not even bridle-paths through the woods. There were only coastal schooners to move things about.

Picture then a piano arriving by schooner at Chester, Nova Scotia. It is a beautiful little instrument, made by Broadwood of London, a gift from Lord Dalhousie, Nova Scotia's Lieutenant Governor, to his friend, Captain William Ross—or rather, to Captain Ross's daughter, Miss Mary Ross.

What a magnificent present! But what a headache it was going to be getting the pres-ent delivered! For Mary Ross and her father did not live in Chester, but some 20 miles away, in the heart of Lunenburg County, at the place which we know today as New Ross. At that time, in 1817, their farm was completely surrounded by deep forest without even a path running through the woods.

Mary Ross's piano

Captain Ross was one of Lord Dalhousie's closest friends and had received a grant of some 13,000 acres which he divided among a colony of several hundred disbanded soldiers from the Napoleonic wars. They formed a militia company with Captain Ross as their leader. It was a lovely place to live, with peaceful, unpolluted lakes and virgin forest-lands. The only trouble was that they had to carry all their supplies in from Chester. And now they were faced with the problem of carrying in a piano.

When word got to New Ross that this piano had been landed on the wharf at Chester, Captain Ross put it up to his men. Did they wish to hear some of their favourite tunes, and some of the latest tunes? Lord Dalhousie must have sent books of music along with the instrument, including some of the newly-introduced Christmas carols. Four soldiers volunteered to go to Chester and bring the piano back with them. They carried it all the way to New Ross, about 20 miles through the woods.

Today, Mary Ross's piano can be seen at the Ross Farm which is operated by the Nova Scotia Museum.

The Ross Farm is open on winter weekends. The children can enjoy the animals and visit them in their snug winter quarters in the barn. If there is plenty of snow they can go on an old-fashioned sleigh ride.

Afterwards, the farm house will be warm and there will be spiced punch simmering on the stove and maybe gingerbread in the oven. Look around the house and, in the parlour, imagine the Ross family standing around their new piano as Mary strikes up the chord for "It Came Upon a Midnight Clear."

"Four soldiers volunteered to go to Chester and bring the piano back... all the way to New Ross, about 20 miles through the woods."

CHRISTMAS EVE IN A SMALL TOWN

"... the soldiers will be able to attend the midnight service at St. Andrew's Anglican Church..."

I would like to tell you how one town in the Maritimes is going to celebrate Christmas Eve. This is my own home town of Hantsport, N.S., which as the name implies, is a port and a very busy one. It is only a small place, with about 2,000 people, but we all have work to do. We have a certain amount of money to spend, and at this season of the year we like to spend it.

Of course our opportunities for spending money are not spectacular. There are no drinking places, none of those cocktail lounges or dimly-lit bars, where you peer in at the vague outlines of lonely folk nursing a martini. The nearest thing we have to a cocktail lounge is the restaurant on Main Street, where you can have coffee at the table beside the window and look out at the people passing by. They can look right back in and see you, and nod if they happen to know you,

which they generally do.

We have no nightclubs, either, with entertainers and that kind of thing. But we do have singing. On Christmas Eve, the young people will be singing carols under the windows of shut-ins while women will be delivering the baskets which they have been busy packing to those who, because of age or illness, can not get out.

The liveliest singing of all will be in the humming wires and clicking relays of the telephone building opposite the garage. Messages will be coming through, from a niece in Vancouver and cousins in Sault Ste. Marie. The singing on those frosty wires makes a very happy chorus on Christmas Eve.

I wish you could see our decorations. Not that yours aren't lovely too but ours are a little bit different. You see, Hantsport is a loading point for the fleet of gypsum boats that shuttle back and forth between here and New York. Sometimes they go to Baltimore, or Jacksonville, New Orleans and Kingston, Jamaica. Some of the crew members live right here in town—or rather, their families live here. They have made sure that those outside decorations can be seen from away down the Bay because, on Christmas Eve, the men will be out on deck watching for the illuminated trees on the front lawn and the electric star up on the roof, as they steam in past Cape Blomidon and on to the Fairway Buoy.

"...the illuminated trees on the front lawn..." Shown at Norm's home, Hantsport, N.S.

At the dock to greet the boat will be rows of cars, their headlights flashing out a welcome from the wives and sweethearts of crew members from out of town. They may have driven up from Halifax, from Liverpool, and even from Yarmouth, 150 miles away, just to be here when the boat comes in.

She will be in port for only two hours, while 10,000 tons of gypsum pour into her hold. Then she blows three times and the car horns on the dock answer, wishing her a good trip. At the final blast, the hawsers are thrown free and she's off again to Baltimore.

What the men look forward to is the "trip off" every two months. It means a five or six day shore leave, to get acquainted with the baby and meet the neighbours.

Of course Christmas Day is celebrated aboard ship. It is a holiday. The men just stand their watch, but there is no work to do out on deck. Then, at two o'clock, they sit down to a bang-up dinner—turkey, roast duck, baked ham, anything you want. Unlike the old windjammer days of salt herring and plum duff, these boys have a choice of roast beef and ice cream, Florida oranges and hearts of celery. But none of them would choose to be on the ship on Christmas Day if there was any way of getting ashore, short of "paying off," quitting the job.

I hope some of them have this trip off, so they can spend the holiday week at home and take part in those crucial last-minute decisions. Will we have the ham hot or cold? Does the silver need cleaning? Should we stuff the turkey tonight or leave it until tomorrow morning? Are you supposed to put onions in the dressing, or is that only for stuffed goose?

If the boat comes in before eleven thirty at night, the sailors will be able to attend the midnight service at St. Andrew's Anglican Church and join in the singing of "While Shepherds Watch Their Flock By Night," and then, at midnight, "Christians Awake, Salute the Happy Morn."

I talked once with a man who could recall when Christmas morning was truly a miracle. His memory went back to the turn of the century, to a time when a strong man might earn a dollar and twenty cents a day cutting firewood—if he could cut a cord and a half. There were few Christmas presents then, but the expectation of that night was so great— the feeling that something miraculous was about to happen—that some of them would tip-toe out to the barn to see if it was indeed true that the cattle were kneeling in their stalls.

All that is gone now. We no longer believe such tales. And yet, as we listen to the bells chiming at midnight, we still anticipate that something wonderful is waiting for us, to be revealed on Christmas morning. What will it be? It can come in such a simple package; a pair of hand-knit socks, some homemade raspberry preserves, or a loaf of strudelbread, frosted in red and green, baked by a friend who learned from her grandmother in Lunenburg how strudelbread is made.

So that is our Christmas Eve. It may not be quite as exciting as in Halifax or Saint John or Charlottetown, but the same expectations are here. We'll all have our lights on over the front door, waiting for someone to come.

So let's bring out a bottle of our home-made blackberry wine, that we may propose a toast. May *your* miracle come true—and may your Christmas be a happy one.

"...Hantsport is a loading point for the fleet of gypsum boats..."

A TREE AT PEGGYS

Peggy's Cove, N.S. with "...a lighthouse that is the most sketched...on the Atlantic seaboard."

It is no good telling myself that Christmas is only for children. I've tried that but it only makes things worse. It simply means you end up the day before Christmas without a tree—with a whole whack of ornaments and bubbling lights and things you've bought at the last moment, and nothing to hang them on.

Every year it's the same thing. I have to dig out the hand axe, start off up the railroad track, and join this little straggling band of last minute celebrants, making a pilgrimage to the woods... then plunge down over the railroad embankment...start searching for a tree that isn't too big, or too small...or too crooked... or the wrong species.

I am quite proud of the one I dragged home this year. It may be a little skimpy in spots, but you don't notice that with the bad side to the wall. Anyway, the main thing is to have the lights on, so they cast a pool of glistening colour on the snow just outside the window, and add to all the other lights along the street this evening.

But suppose now, suppose you were not in this snug little home of yours. Suppose that tonight you were out at sea, on a tossing trawler, facing into the murky North Atlantic. How good it would be to catch a glimpse of those Christmas lights, glowing from some lonely headland—perhaps on Candlebox Island, among the Tuskets, off Yarmouth County, or one of the other Tusket Islands. There is not a tree growing there to bless its name, because of the sheep that have grazed them, but there'll be a tree there tonight, surely, even though it's meant a special trip to the mainland. And out on Sable Island, where nothing much taller than grass can grow, there must be a tree in somebody's window. The lookouts are watching for it. The revolving flash of a lighthouse isn't a beacon enough for tonight. There are other messages to be flashed out across the dark.

Along the coast from Halifax, at Peggys Cove, the trees have never grown beyond a few stunted, wind-blown spruce. It is not easy to find a Christmas tree at Peggys. It never has been. You have to tramp a long ways back from the shore, crawling about among the boulders, to chop down a tree that's worthy of tonight.

But they've found them—beautiful trees too, reaching all the way to the ceiling—and decorated with lights that shine out over the frothing ice surf, along with the beam from a lighthouse that is the most sketched, the most painted lighthouse on the Atlantic seaboard.

I know there are trees at Peggys tonight because of a poem I chanced upon in a chapbook of the Nova Scotia Poetry Society—a poem that told me what kind of people live in Peggys Cove.

You have probably been to Peggys. You will have wandered about among the fish sheds, out on the wharves, and watched the artists at work, sketching the men as they unload their boats or hang their nets up to dry. There are so many wonderful pictures you can get at Peggys, even if you aren't an artist—pictures you can store away in your mind's eye of this very strange natural phenomenon. It is a place swept clean of every vestige of soil and vegetation, a place that is compounded of nothing but the two elemental sources of all life—rock and water. Among this primordial desolation are little houses perched within spray distance of the pounding, remorseless sea.

The people at Peggys have for generations been fishermen. But their cove is such an unusual one, that it has become over the years, the very symbol of every fishing village along Nova Scotia's rugged South Shore. Thousands of tourists drive out to Peggys every summer to watch the sea gulls, wander about among the boulders (some of them as big as a house), peer in at the fish sheds, and in a hundred other ways invade the privacy of this little village. Yet the people at Peggys Cove allow themselves to be sketched and painted, and when the cameras click, they just smile and go about their work.

Then, as autumn skies turn the sea from sparkling blue to leaden grey, the visitors depart and leave the people at Peggys to enjoy a little peace and quiet for the winter months. At Christmas, they begin receiving cards from all the friends they've made last summer...and the summer before.

But about this poem: it was written by E. Mildred Atwood of Halifax. Mrs. Atwood, who was born in Lunenburg County, at New Ross, attended the Halifax School for the Blind. When she went to Peggys Cove, she "saw" something beyond the lighthouse and the killocks, and the fish flakes. She heard the voices of the people who live at Peggys; she felt the warmth of their handshake; she caught the fragrance of a genial hospitality. The people in her poem are all real people and that's what I like about it. It seems to

At Peggy's Cove "you have to tramp a long way back from the shore...for a tree..."

bring you into their very homes, so that you almost share their fireside.

Remember that the poem was written when fishing was still the principal occupation of Peggys. It is no longer. The three or four boats that still go out are equipped with such sophisticated fishing gear that one would hardly refer to such men as "simple fisher folk," but I am sure that when Mrs. Atwood wrote this poem, many years ago, she meant it as a compliment.

If you go down to Peggy's Cove
*   To sketch the waters blue,*
Some kindly fisher family
*   Will surely welcome you.*
The heavy seines and lighthouse,
*   Fish drying on the flakes,*
Could never hold your interest,
*   Like the meal that Nellie makes.*

The poet writes at Peggy's Cove,
*   And pictures in his rhymes*
The warrior King Atlantic
*   As he rules the Maritimes.*
But all the tales of shipwreck,
*   Which makes his worthy books,*
Could never cheer the spirit
*   Like a chat with Grandma Crooks.*

If you go down to Peggy's Cove,
*   To woo the wind and waves,*
The little church around the bend,
*   Holds all the grace that saves.*
But you may find sweet Charity
*   As round the rocks you rove,*
Among the simple fisher folk,
*   That dwell at Peggy's Cove.*

Isn't that a charming picture? It is a very good reason to believe that tonight there will be trees at Peggys Cove.

RECOLLECTIONS OF CHRISTMAS PAST, HALLS HARBOUR

The snow seemed to come earlier in those years and there was more of it. It eddied down silently out of the grey December skies and spread like a rising tide along the country roads until it formed a nightcap on the fence posts. The little houses huddled closer and closer to the barn and to the wood-shed and root-cellar. The old man would come out into the yard, look up and down the road, and go back into the house and say, "Afraid you won't get that parcel before Christmas. There's no sign of the mailman this morning. He won't be through for a week now."

That is the way it was in those days. There were miles and miles of country roads without a footprint, one village cut off from another for months on end, with a few stubborn men facing into the wind with nothing but a shovel in their mittened hands, the frost clinging to their whiskers. No sooner would they clear the road than it would all drift in again.

On the Bay of Fundy shore, between Digby and Scotts Bay, N.S., the winds swept in across the water all the way from Saint John, N.B., and beat against the lighthouse windows. The drifts were high in Parkers Cove, Port Lorne, Margaretsville, and Halls Harbour. Sometimes they did not leave their homes all winter. Was it lonely? Well, let's see what it was like.

A friend of mine, who was a toddler at the turn of the century, has given me her recollections of a childhood Christmas in the home of her grandfather at Halls Harbour.

It began weeks and weeks before Christmas day. It began, as a matter of fact, after the big storm that blew all the driftwood up on shore. The men would take their cross-cut saws and go down along the beach to junk up the bigger pieces so they could be hauled up into the door-yard by ox-team. Grandfather would say, "You can't beat driftwood. It gives the best heat for cooking. The salt's bad on the grates, but it's the only fire for roasting a goose."

A few weeks later, Grandfather would take a trip over to Saint John. He went over on a little coastal vessel—not the coastal steamer *Ruby L.*; she was to come later. This was a little sailing ship. When he returned from Saint John he brought with him the winter's supplies—barrels of flour and sugar, both white and brown, molasses, corn meal, baking soda, and kerosene oil for the lamps.

As soon as the weather grew frosty enough, Grandmother set to work in earnest, cooking. You didn't wait till a few days before the holiday and then rush out to the store to buy something. Oh dear, no! Gradually, over the weeks, you built up an armoury of Christmas goodies which were stored away in a downstairs bedroom that nobody used. It was as cold as a refrigerator, and just the place for storing mince pies, railroad cakes, tarts filled with gooseberry jelly, and homemade sausage. These were not sausages the way we have them today. They were little round patties, like hamburgers, and these were piled up on big blue and white platters.

Halls Harbour, N.S.

Now these preparations went on for weeks, and for a very good reason. Grandmother knew perfectly well that, snowdrifts or no snowdrifts, the other branches of the family, from up on the Mountain, and along the Bay Shore, would be arriving on Christmas morning and would stay for the best part of a week. She had *better* have something in that spare bedroom.

There was also a personal reason. Among the Christmas visitors would be the *other* Grandmother, and between these two grandmothers there existed a fierce rivalry as to which could serve up the most overwhelming, the most stupendous mounds of irresistible delicacies—individual mince pies (as well as standard size), plum pudding, with a very special sweet butter sauce, and, in a big glass bowl kept from year to year for this very purpose, Grandmother's wild strawberry preserves.

During these days leading up to Christmas, the girls were given the use of a spare room off the dining room, equipped with a little Franklyn wood-burning stove. Here they sat, with their feet on the fender, toasting their shins and making Christmas presents—a spool-box of grey linen, painted with snowdrops, a calendar for the coming year, with "1905" printed in goldleaf and "Greetings from Halls Harbour," a magazine rack, a whisk broom holder, and all sorts of strange little articles. They had the most wonderful time making them and everyone thought they were simply marvellous.

Then grandmother puts her head in at the door and says, "Now you children have been in here long enough. You'll catch cold, come out into the kitchen and warm yourself and help me stone these raisins." The raisins were soaked overnight, and then "stoned." So now they sat removing the seeds from the raisins, and about every fifth raisin they popped into their mouths—if Grandmother wasn't looking.

In certain activities the children were not allowed to participate. Of course they could not be unaware that Grandfather had cut and hauled in the big fir tree from the far pasture and set it up in the parlour, a dim twilight room with a parlour organ, an abundance of Boston rockers, and a horsehair sofa, a room that had somehow been transformed into an enchanted grotto. The children were warned not to touch the candles which had been fixed to the tree in little holders that snapped onto the outer branches—candles of twisted pink, like votive lights, flickering in the shadows, while the family stood about holding their breath, and hoping the whole thing would not go up in smoke.

As one looks back across the years to that Christmas tree, one can still smell those tiny pink candles, the wax guttering down onto the branches. One can smell, too, the preparations under way in the kitchen where Grandmother is making a dressing for the goose of tart apples, and chopped up onions and sage. On the stove is a saucepan filled with goose oil, which she has strained out from the fat. Next time someone has a cold some of that goose oil will be rubbed on his chest. There is nothing like goose, declares Grandmother. It gives you goose oil for medicine and down to stuff your mattress and your pillows. The wing, with the feathers left in it, makes a fine feather duster.

When Grandfather comes in and sees the Christmas tree with the candles still lighted, he says, "Now that's enough, blow them out. You'll have them burned down to the heel. It's time you children went to bed. Off with you now. We'll light them tomorrow after the family gets here. Wait till you hear your aunt and your uncle coming in the butterboat sleigh, with the bells jingling, and down on the floor, all your cousins peeking out from under the Buffalo robe. Wait till *they* get here...."

"Wait 'till you hear your aunt and uncle coming in the... sleigh, with...all your cousins..."

RECOLLECTIONS OF CHRISTMAS PAST, THE GASPEREAU VALLEY

Imagine Christmas—without any money! We are back in the year 1900. The place is the Gaspereau Valley in Nova Scotia. You are ten years old, growing up on a farm. You have been in to Wolfville once, in the cutaway sleigh, and gaped at the Christmas finery along Main Street, glistening in the store windows. There were toy drums, in red and yellow, china-headed dolls, a railway steam engine with cow-catcher in front, a fire engine, drawn by two white horses, a jack-in-the-box, a rocking horse.

Probably, none of these will be for you. Perhaps the jack-in-the-box, possibly the toy drum; but the rocking horse or the railway locomotive, no. Your parents have not encouraged you to write a letter to Santa Claus, con-fiding that one of these might perhaps interest you. Yet you have a feeling, a restless, breathless intimation, that something spectacular will be there waiting for you on Christmas morning. Else, why did your parents not allow you to accompany them into the general store? They have no money to buy things, of course. You know that. But they do have credit, built up over the months with baskets of eggs, prints of butter, and bags of turnips and potatoes.

The door opens and your father beckons you to come in. You throw back the robe, bound out of the cutter, and next moment you are inside the store, standing beside a hissing beehive stove, surrounded by barrels of fancy biscuits and caddies of tea. The shelves are piled with crockery and yard-

"During the long drive home, you lie curled up on the floor of the cutter..."

The Gaspereau Valley, N.S.

goods, and on the counter is a rounded glass case filled with candy.

Your mother hands you an egg. You, in turn, pass this egg on to the merchant, who now indicates that you may pick out any candy in the case. What a choice! There are saw logs, six inches long, in solid peppermint, chocolate tents, with cream centres, and conversational lozenges: "You are my sweetheart"; "Can I see you home tonight?" in the most poisonous shades of pink, yellow, and purple.

During the long drive home, you lie curled up on the floor of the cutter, under the buffalo robe, chewing on your peppermint saw log, listening to the chiming of the horse bells, dreaming of all the wonders you have seen, and speculating if Santa Claus might bring you a pair of larrigans, as he did last year to the two boys who live on the farm halfway up the mountain. They each received a pair of larrigans and a pole axe! They could hardly wait for Christmas dinner to be over before they were out tramping back to the woodlot, to try out their new axes.

Then you begin thinking of Christmas dinner. There will be mince pies. The very choicest of mince pies, made with rabbit meat from rabbits you caught yourself back on the mountain, because everyone knows that rabbits make the best mincemeat.

Your mind is irresistibly drawn back to those strange-shaped parcels your father has stowed away in the back of the cutter. What will they contain? You are on the verge of reaching back to see if you can touch them, when the cutter suddenly stops. You look out from under the robe and here you are on the river road, almost back home, alongside the neighbour's mail box. Your mother hands you a cup and gives you careful instructions. There is baking to be done today and she will have to borrow a cupful of seed yeast from her neighbour's supply, to start off a fresh batch. This will be poured into the big stone two gallon yeast jug, and placed beside the kitchen stove to ferment. Of course she will return the cupful later on, when her neighbour's yeast jug begins to run out. By the time you get home with the yeast, the mysterious parcels have been whisked off into the house and are nowhere to be seen.

Already your mother is at work seeding raisins, for she now has some kidney suet she got at the store. Only beef kidney suet, the very best, will do for a plum pudding. Everyone gathers about to take a hand. Each member of the family gives the pudding a stir, for good luck. But first, Grandpa must recite the riddle, the traditional jingle which he teases us with every year.

Flour of England, fruit of Spain,
Met together in a shower of rain.
Put in a bag, tied around with a string,
If you tell me this riddle I'll give you a ring.

The answer, of course, is a plum pudding. When the pudding is cooked, your mother takes the pudding bag, washes it out, dries it carefully and stores it away in the pantry for next year.

Is there to be a Christmas tree? Perhaps, but not likely. The Christmas tree was brought to Canada not too many years before, in 1846, by a German woman who married Mr. William Pryor of Halifax. This was the first Canadian Christmas tree, and though the custom spread rapidly, there are still many homes, in 1900, where it is frowned on, par-ticularly in communities with a Puritan back-ground—and the people of Gaspereau Valley originally came from New England.

But there are decorations! You and your brothers and sisters have been busy for days making tissue paper chains, wreaths of ground juniper for the window, decked out with wild holly berries, and crowned with a homemade tallow candle. You have been doing immense things with pine cones. These were painted with ordinary house paint, red, green, and white, and frosted with sugar and salt before the paint hardened.

Grandpa watched benignly over all this activity from his rocker beside the wood-burn-ing kitchen stove. Every so often he lighted his pipe and, as this was Christmastime, Mother offered him a match from the book of wooden matches she had purchased at the store, matches tipped with sulphur. But he shook his head. Grandpa prefers his own self-made spills. He keeps a supply of these on the mantel, and after he has lighted his pipe with one, he leans over, snuffs it out among the ashes, and returns it to the mantel for future use. He sits there with his jackknife, fretting pieces of wood into the most curious shapes. Whatever is he making?

"...you know there is a long winter ahead to play with all those toys."

At last it is Christmas morning. Now you know that Grandpa has been busy making a dancing man—a little wooden man with jointed limbs, hanging from a cord strung between two poles, who will dance for you when you give a rhythmic touch to the cord.

There are other presents too, most of them home-made: hand sleds, a little wheelbarrow, a tiny dump car, a pair of spring skates. Then, for girls, there are pinafores, stocking caps and mittens and a yellow hair ribbon for one, blue for the other.

On Christmas Eve you hung up your stocking, not forgetting to set out a plate with an apple on it, for Santa to give to his reindeer, because nothing sustains reindeer like an apple grown in the Gaspereau Valley.

In that stocking, this morning, you found an orange, an openwork bag of gumdrops, a tiger or an elephant made of clear candy in yellow or red, and a toy: for the boys a tin whistle, for the girls a rag doll.

Your presents occupy you completely all morning until you hear the oven door being opened…and there sits the goose, the hot fat sizzling in the pan, the smell of sage dressing perfuming the air.

"…Grandpa has been busy making a dancing man…"

Not only is there a goose, but the roast of pork as well, with apple sauce to go with it—all grown on the home farm.

As your father carves the goose, everyone watches to see the state of the keel bone—a most important and urgent matter, this business of the keel bone. For if the keel bone is white it means a heavy winter lies ahead, with much snow. But if the keel bone is partly white and partly dark, you can look forward to an open winter and an early spring.

Whichever colour it is, you know there are plenty of supplies stored away in the cellar, and a long winter ahead to play with all those toys. You will learn to skate on your new spring skates—and who needs any money?

TOO MUCH OF A GOOD THING

"...the gutter...was aflow with the finest imported liquors."

Money is great stuff to have around, of course, when you need it. But do you suppose there is such a thing as having too much money? The oil tycoon, J. Paul Getty, who owned the controlling interest in 200 businesses, was said to be worth four billion dollars. But, for all his billions, J. Paul Getty never felt secure and, in 1957, sadly philosophized that, "a billion dollars isn't worth what it used to be." He just had too much of a good thing.

Or take those intellectual attainments which some people consider even more important than money itself. Even here you can be a little *too* good.

The English historian, Thomas Babington Macaulay, was not only a brilliant writer but a great talker as well. He was perhaps better at making speeches than after-dinner conversation, which is an art in itself. At one dinner party, Macaulay held the floor for something like half an hour. Towards the end of this monologue, an old gentleman leaned over and whispered to his neighbour, "Sir, his information is greater than society requires."

Too much of anything can turn what should be a pleasure into a matter of complaint. This once happened with the people of Saint John, N.B., who developed a snob- bish distaste for perfectly good mahogany furniture. It came about like this.

In the early days of sailing ships, Saint John's waterfront supported a fleet of ships trading with the West Indies. On the trip down south they carried cargoes of dried fish, lumber, potatoes. When they returned, in the hold, as ballast, they sometimes carried mahogany logs—green mahogany logs which are extremely heavy. Once they had tied up at Saint John, the logs were unloaded and tossed to one side, just to get rid of them. Anyone who wanted some mahogany logs was welcome to carry them off home. Naturally the cabinet makers of Saint John helped themselves to these logs and produced furniture that is today found for the most part only in museums. At that time, nobody knew they were masterpieces. You could buy mahogany chairs very reasonably then, partly, of course, because the furniture makers were getting their raw material for nothing. Finally, it reached a point where the well-to-do would not think of furnishing their homes with mahogany—it was too commonplace and vulgar. In fact we have a letter written by someone visiting one of these well-to-do homes, who says, "It was nice to see that the home was furnished in fancy woods instead of the mahogany which the poor people use." Imagine! Those people in Saint John were just spoiled by too much mahogany.

The people of Prince Edward Island used to look down their noses at lobsters, simply because lobsters were too plentiful. At one time, you could walk down to the shore and pick up two or three off the rocks. After a storm, they were piled up on the beaches five feet deep, lying there on the sand. Anyone could help themselves to lobsters, so that too—like the mahogany chairs of Saint John—became a mark of poverty. If company arrived at your house and caught you eating lobsters you were mortified beyond words. When you got down to eating lobster Newburg, it meant you'd just about struck bottom.

There is hardly anything in the world that doesn't become a problem when you get too much of it—even religion. For example there was Joseph Gaynor of Fredericton, N.B., who

had really got religion—the Methodist religion. That meant that above all else, he was a dedicated teetotaller. It so happened that one of Fredericton's leading merchants had died leaving Joseph Gaynor to act as chief executor. When he came to examine the stock in the warehouse, he found there were dozens of casks of gin, rum, brandy, and wine. What was he to do? He could not allow this merchandise to be sold, to tempt others into the pitfalls of inebriation. No, he would make good for these casks out of his own pocket. They must be destroyed. He rolled them out to the edge of the sidewalk, and there, with an axe, he knocked in the heads. Soon, the gutter on Queen Street was aflow with the finest imported liquors. At this point, a cow owned by Colonel George Minchin came wandering down the street. She was obviously thirsty so took a drink from the gutter. She came back for another drink, and another, continuing unsteadily down the street. Finally, she staggered into an open ditch and landed on top of two men who were digging a sewer—and who became the unwitting victims of the temperance cause.

The story of Colonel Minchin's cow is often told in Fredericton, especially on New Year's Eve, as a cautionary tale, to warn us that, even with so admirable a cause as temperance, there are times when we can have too much of a good thing!

NEW YEAR'S CUSTOMS

Do you believe in astrology? If you do, I hope you have been studying your horoscope, because horoscopes have to do with luck—whether it is our lucky day or our unlucky day. During this Christmas week, it seems as if we are either dodging bad luck or meeting good luck head-on whenever we step outside the house.

"...knocking on doors all over town."

I had no idea, until I started looking into it, what a dangerous time Christmas week can be, or, on the other hand, how much prosperity may be lying just around the corner. It all depends on what you do.

Consider: Among French Canadians, there is a belief that it is unlucky if a cat meows in the house on Christmas Eve. Thus they feed their cats especially well the day before Christmas. This same custom may apply to New Year's Eve as well. So, on December 31, make sure to lay in a good supply of cat chow. No matter how fat your favourite tabby, she just might meow on New Year's Eve. That would not be good.

If you should live in Lunenburg County, N.S., then, for goodness sakes don't forget to oil up the shotgun and buy some blank shells. As you know, if your memories of Lunenburg go back any time at all, when the chimes ring at midnight, you simply have to shoot the old year out, and the new year in. If you don't you just might be in trouble—big trouble.

This custom seems to have been brought to the New World from the Old. Sir James Frazer, writing in his masterpiece *The Golden Bough*, said

...witching time is the twelve days between Christmas and Epiphany. Hence in some parts of Silesia on New Year's Eve they fire shots over fields and meadows, into shrubs and trees, and wrap straw round the fruit-trees, to prevent the spirits from doing them harm. On New Year's Eve, which is Saint Sylvester's Day, Bohemian lads, armed with guns, form themselves into circles and fire thrice into the air. This is called 'Shooting the Witches' and is supposed to frighten the witches away.

Now, in Port Greville, N.S., it is not witches they worry about so much, it's...a red-headed man. In some ways this may be just as bad.

I have heard of people in Port Greville who will go to almost any lengths to prevent a red-headed man from being the first to enter the house on New Year's Day. Believe me, a red-headed man, or even a man whose hair is slightly on the blond side, can just about spoil your whole year. So be sure the first man to enter your house on New Year's Day has dark hair. It could make all the difference.

The first caller on New Year's Day can greatly influence the whole course of your life. In Pictou, N.S., if you happen to be an unmarried woman, the first man entering the house on New Year's Day will become your husband. I just hope he isn't red-headed.

In my own home town of Hantsport this is called "first footing," only they don't bother with the marrying part. It simply gives the lucky man the privilege of kissing all the ladies. I've known friends of mine who could hardly wait till breakfast was over

before they were out knocking on doors all over town.

But then, on New Year's Day, there is so much good luck going, it is pretty hard to avoid, especially if you should live along the North Shore of New Brunswick, or on the Digby Shore, where the old Acadian traditions of hospitality can still be met in a glass of wine and some Christmas cake—with a happy month for every piece of cake you eat. You might even be offered that most famous of Acadian dishes, Rappie Pie. This consists of potatoes, grated in a very special manner, and then put in a baking dish. First there is a layer of potatoes, then a layer of some sort of meat—chicken or turkey, or even clams, or mussels—and then another layer of potatoes. This is put in the oven to bake and if it doesn't give you a lucky month, nothing will.

What I like about this time of year are those footsteps in the fresh-fallen snow up to

"No matter how fat your favorite tabby, she just might meow..."

"The first caller on New Year's day can greatly influence...your life."

lonely houses that are seldom visited but are never forgotten on New Year's Day.

The best wish of all, I think, is the one you'll hear in Old Scotland, "Lang may your lum reek." It simply means; "Long may your chimney smoke." Yet, despite all these good wishes for our health and prosperity, this Christmas week can be a very dangerous one.

We have a fish man who comes around in a truck every week and calls in at each house along the street. When he came yesterday he said,

"Well, I won't be calling in for the next two weeks."

"Oh", I said, "you're staying home for the holiday."

"No," he said, "I'm staying home because nobody's buying any fish. What's the good of coming around? Everybody's got so much turkey, and chicken, and mince pies. They're not bothering with fish. And some of them have been overdoing it a bit. They're too sick to even answer the door...."

So there you have a few words from my fish man; just a reminder to take it easy. And in the meantime..."Lang may your lum reek."

◈

"...you simply have to shoot the old year out..."

WRECKERS AND THE YEAR
OF THE SECOND CHRISTMAS

In the chancy, blustering days of sailing ships, every fishing village along Nova Scotia's rugged South Shore experienced the grim saga of the ship that went on the rocks. Wrecks were commonplace.

Today, with radar and other electronic devices, we hardly ever hear of a ship going on the rocks; but when she does, the stakes are high. She may be carrying five or six thousand tons of readily marketable goods. If her hatches are still above water, she will soon be surrounded by dories and motor launches from within a radius of 30 miles.

The men in these little boats are known as "wreckers." Belying this sinister name, they turn out to be a group of quite reputable and law-abiding fishermen; in fact, along the rocky shores out at the head of Halifax harbour, the fishermen would respond almost to a man if the news went out that a ship had gone on the rocks.

However, they feel that a wreck piled up on the reefs, and still above water, is the sea's way of compensating them for the hardship it so often visits on these little fishing villages. So they jump in their boats and start off for the wreck and, when they get there, they circle about her cautiously, sizing up just how safe it is to go aboard. It is this hazard of the game that makes it so exciting and attracts those with the spirit of adventure.

One of the most famous of these wrecks was an American freighter loaded with supplies for the American troops overseas—the

"The men in these little boats are known as 'wreckers'."

Untitled watercolour by Alan Creighton

Martin Van Buren. In January of 1945, she was attacked by a U-boat just outside Halifax harbour and appeared to be sinking. Captain and crew abandoned her and took to the boats.

As it turned out, the *Martin Van Buren* was not sinking. She drifted off into heavy fog which set in after a snow storm. With nobody aboard, this rudderless ship managed somehow to make her way safely through the jagged rocks of the Sambro Ledge until reaching shore.

At 5 o'clock on the morning of January 15, a fisherman heard a loud grating noise off shore. It wasn't until that afternoon that someone glimpsed, through the fog, the large ship lying broadside, not more than 500 feet from land. At that point Santa Claus took over, with a distribution of largess that is talked about in places like Sambro even to this day.

By late afternoon, word had spread along the coast some 25 miles in each direction, and soon the boats started coming—motor boats, cabin cruisers, Cape Islanders, and just plain old-fashioned row boats.

"...wooden boxes out of the hold... containing wartime rations..."

"...everyone was hastening up off the shore to hide their burlap bag..."

Already, the venturesome had thrown a line up over the side and climbed aboard. Now they were handing wooden boxes up out of the hold—boxes containing wartime rations for the American Army, cans of beef stew, frankfurters and beans, grapefruit juice, pineapple juice, gallon tins of fruit cocktail, along with Hershey chocolate bars, and cartons of cigarettes (Lucky Strike, Raleigh, Camel and Philip Morris). Here, help yourself. It's Christmas once again!

For many, this second Christmas came as a godsend. Butter, tea, and sugar could not be bought without coupons in the final months of the war. Even unrationed goods were in short supply—such household necessities as soap—and here they were handing out hundreds of boxes of a "toilet goods accessory package," containing toothpaste, two tubes of Barbasol, five tubes of Cabot shaving cream, and 14 small cakes of Camay soap. What would Santa think of next?

As the wreckers brought their boatloads of goodies ashore, they were met by a line of customers on the beach. There were truckers

"...soon the boats started coming– motor boats, cabin cruisers, Cape Islanders..."

from Halifax, taxi drivers, people eager for food items to vary the wartime rations, girls looking for soap and cigarettes—four cartons (800 cigarettes) for two dollars.

Everything was going along just fine with people laughing and comparing notes and wondering what new delights lay in the holds of the *Martin Van Buren*. Then, like a thunderclap, came word that the Mounties were on their way with orders to confiscate all this contraband.

Suddenly, everyone was hastening up off the shore to hide their burlap bag behind some rocks, or stow it under the back seat of the car, or cache it in a secret spot in the woods, or give it away to anyone they happened to meet along the beach, just so they would not be lugging a sack of this stuff by the time the Mounties got there.

The Mounties set up a road block on the outskirts of Halifax, at Spryfield, and captured a few bags of shaving cream and cigarettes and grapefruit juice. But a great deal of this luxury cargo found its way into the city

and was sold on the black market. It spread out, in fact, far beyond Halifax. In the Annapolis Valley, one noticed that suddenly everyone was smoking Lucky Strikes and there was a great increase in gum-chewing (20 packets to a carton).

Then the Mounties started poking about, searching for contraband. One farmer had a very unhappy experience. He'd been doing a lively business in hard cider, which he sold to the right customers for two dollars a gallon. One day, he got wind that the Mounties were in the neighbourhood, searching barns and cellars. Without bothering to find out what they were actually looking for, he emptied 500 gallons of the very best sparkling cider into the pig-pen. That was a real wartime tragedy.

❖

THE SHANTY CREW

You spend the day outdoors in air that sparkles with frost and is spiced with pine needles and hemlock balsam. You sit down to a heaping plate of baked beans and salt fat pork—and call for more. At day's end your straw tick is a grateful prelude to dreamland. You are working in a lumber camp.

There is a man here in my home town who has a perfectly good steady job, but throughout the winter he spends his weekly free day off working in a lumber camp about six miles out in the woods. It's his winter tonic.

So what is it like out in these lumber camps? Well, if you are determined to come along, remember one thing, Cook is the boss of the shanty. What Cook says in the bunkhouse is law. He'll give you more than ginger bread if you start making a nuisance of yourself, and gabbing after nine o'clock. When he says, "Lights out"...you turn that light out, brother, and stop talking.

Remember, he has to roll out long before daylight—four o'clock, in fact—to rebuild his fire, put the kettle on, start making tea. He is not going to stand for any of this gay, madcap business of staying up after nine. Besides, if you are one of the teamsters he will be calling you at five in the morning, so that you can go out and feed your horses. If you are one of the choppers, he'll roust you out at six. So you had better figure to be in that bunk by nine o'clock. Okay?

And oh, yes, about cards; it is not that he objects to a game of Penny Ante, to while away the evening, but if anyone starts acting

"...the men do not stay in camp all winter the way they used to."

up kind of ugly, inclined to curse a little too much perhaps—sort of sharp and raspy—don't worry, Cook will soon step in. "Give me those cards. If you don't know how to enjoy yourselves, there'll be no more card playing in this shanty until you learn to act like men."

That is Cook—boss of the camp. What he says in the bunkhouse goes. And you daren't say a word back to him or he'll give you your walking ticket. Just take it easy and watch your manners. No talking at mealtimes! It only holds things up, and he has enough to do, serving up roast beef, and baked beans, pork and sauerkraut, homemade apple pies, white cake, and homemade bread. No one ever leaves the table hungry.

Then, after supper, come on, strike up a tune on the mouth organ! Let's have some tap dancing, or a song that has been sung for a good many years in the lumber camps of Nova Scotia.

Come all ye jolly lumbermen
And listen to my song.
It's all about the shanty crew
And how they get along.
It's all about the shanty crew,
So jolly and so fine.
They spend the lonesome winter
Getting down the pine.

The evenings pass quickly enough, with songs and the swapping of stories. Some of the men have been to sea, while others are farmers. Some have worked at the race tracks, another is a blacksmith. They sit around and yarn and play cards. One man has a sliver in his ax handle and he scrapes the handle down with his knife. Then he keeps on scraping, to thin the neck of the handle down, to give the ax more spring, so that it cuts like something almost alive. Pretty soon Cook says, "Now see here, Bill, you clean that mess up, I'm not sweeping up any more of your shavings. And listen, if you fellas are gonna chew tobacco, the stove is over there."

Then comes nine o'clock and "lights out." The bunkhouse lies in darkness. Nothing is heard but the crackling of the stove. A thread of smoke trickles from the roof-jack up into the night sky. Overhead, a crescent moon looks down on the clearing. An owl hoots and away off another answers.

Of course, the men do not stay in camp all winter the way they used to. Nowadays they go home for the weekends. And oddly enough, when they come out of the woods, they find it chilly back in town with folks scurrying along wind-blown streets huddled up in their fleece-lined overcoats, peeking out from under parka hoods. It all looks so terribly cold—and it feels cold too. It is not in the least the way it is out here in the woods. Here the wind howls high in the branches, and down where you are chopping it is quiet. Crisp, frosty, yes—but somehow you feel warm, as you look up to survey this great encompassing blanket that protects you from the raw cut of the wind.

In a stand of timber, most of the trees are only beginning to put on growth. Others are mature and ready for harvesting. These are the ones to be cut down, and after they have been felled, they must be hauled out to the main road. This is where the horse—and the ox—is still invaluable. A narrow passageway through the forest is hacked out to the fallen tree, just wide enough to allow the horse to squeeze through. This is a called a snig road. The horse snigs, or hauls, the log out to the brow, which is a big pile of logs, high enough that they can be rolled by gravity onto a truck, and then taken away to the mill.

The men work as a team, each depending on the other to know his job in situations where ignorance or bungling can never be tolerated. It is work that is not easy, not too safe, but to any man who has once become a lumberman there is no other job that can be as deeply satisfying. In the years ahead, no matter where you are, no matter how far your career may lead you, during the winter months, there will always be a part of you that longs to return again to the lumber woods.

◆

"...a big pile of logs...taken away to the mill."

DUSTY, THE LUMBER CAMP DOG

A lumber camp dog is a dog without a home. Everybody is his friend but nobody is his master. Some dogs are never happy until they've found someone they can depend on—someone to take them for walks, to throw a stick for them and make sure they get a bone or two now and then.

Dusty got plenty to eat; the men were always handing him titbits. But he could never be sure which one was his master. That was the problem.

When it came springtime and the lumber camp started breaking up, he stood hopefully by, wagging his tail as, one by one, the men began packing their suitcases and donning their mackinaws.

Some of them left without even saying good-bye. Others gave him an absent-minded pat, and then they were gone. It began to look mighty lonesome in that camp. Cook was washing up the last of the dishes and tossed him some scraps but Dusty didn't have any appetite for pork chops. He was beginning to wonder whether people were as good as he'd thought they were.

When Cook finally got through with the broom, he swept Dusty outdoors, picked up his suitcase, snapped a padlock on the door and started walking down the path that led to the lake. Dusty had been down to the lake a few times but it was all frozen over and most of the cottages along the shore were locked up. It looked as if people didn't come there in the wintertime.

There was one cottage that gave out a smell of balsam fir from the wood-smoke drifting away from the chimney. The door was opened before Cook had even knocked, by a man Dusty had seen once or twice up at the camp. "You got a leash so I can tie him up?" the man asked.

"No," said Cook, "you don't need no leash. He won't run away. He wouldn't know where to run to."

"Dusty...tore back to the house with the paper in his mouth."

"Okay," said the man, "it's up to him if he wants to stay. He can sleep out in the woodhouse."

"That's just great," said Cook. "Thanks for taking him off my hands. Didn't want to put him out of the way."

Dusty did not know quite what to make of this conversation, except he did not care for that last remark of Cook's and he was glad to see him walking back up the path through the woods. Now he could give his full attention to this man who was going to let him stay here.

"Well," said the man, "come on inside if you're comin'. I'll see if there's something to eat."

It sounded like a pretty good beginning. As things turned out Dusty had never known anything like it. He now had a real home. It was a home where he could lie down under the stove and groan with contented warmth after a full meal.

Dusty wanted to make sure that it stayed that way. So he began chasing through the woods, trying to round up something to bring home to present to his master for dinner—but the rabbits always got away. He couldn't even catch a spruce partridge. The

"...the conductor on the Dayliner...tossed a newspaper out of the window..."

plain fact was that Dusty's pedigree was a little mixed up. Part of him wanted to chase rabbits and the other part of him just wanted to run through the woods and enjoy himself. He was never able to bring anything home to show how much he appreciated being there. Then, one afternoon, something happened that changed his whole life.

The cottage where he was living, although it was way out in the woods, was right beside the railroad—the Dominion Atlantic Railway that runs between Yarmouth and Halifax. It is a little place called Stillwater, or Stillwater Lake, between Ellershouse and Mount Uniacke. Dusty had got into the habit of chasing after the train, the Dayliner, every day.

One afternoon, the conductor on this train, saw Dusty coming out to meet the train. He tossed a newspaper out of the window—a paper he'd just finished reading. Dusty pounced on it as if he'd flushed a wild duck or uncovered a covey of quail and tore back to the house with the paper in his mouth. His master was delighted to have the newspaper delivered right to his door. It saved him a trip into Windsor.

Next day the conductor and the engineer repeated the same performance. This time Dusty tried to catch the newspaper but it hit him on the side of the head, so, after that, he was careful not to get too close. But he was always there waiting for the Dayliner and its crew. (He knew when to expect them because just before they got there they'd give two sharp little toots on the whistle.)

This went on for about a year until the retirement of the engineer on the afternoon train. Shortly after that the conductor was transferred from the afternoon run to the morning run so there was nobody left on the afternoon Dayliner to throw Dusty a paper. Dusty began once again to wonder if human beings just weren't dependable.

When the conductor realized that nobody on the afternoon train was doing anything to see that Dusty got the latest news, he started throwing a paper from the morning train.

By this time two of the girls at the canteen in the CN Station in Halifax began to be involved. They put aside a paper for Dusty every day and tied it up neatly with two pieces of string so he could carry it in his mouth without damaging the headlines.

If you take that trip on the Dayliner, between Halifax and Kentville, as I did the other day, ask the conductor to let you know when they're approaching Stillwater. You'll hear two toots on the whistle from the engineer and within moments, you'll see the daily paper sailing through the air, and Dusty waiting to grab it and tear back to the house with the morning's news.

Dusty's pretty happy with his new home. And he must sometimes think, there's nothing like living on the right side of the tracks.

◆

HER MAJESTY'S
VERY SPECIAL DELIVERY

You've read about people who sit at home cooped up in their room, never coming out, never talking to anyone, getting to be real hermits? The city is full of people like that. You will find them out in the country, too, but not in the little towns. The little towns have a most marvellous institution for keeping us all well and happy. It's called the Post Office.

You see, in my home town we don't have postal delivery service the way you do, in the city and out in the rural areas. We just have the Post Office. We have to go and get our own mail. Our Post Office makes absolutely no effort to help us. We are completely on our own. It assumes that men, and even women, are capable of walking two or three blocks and tottering home under the weight of a mail order catalogue.

"...at the top are the smaller boxes...for the average citizen..."

It's hard to be a hermit if you have to go and get your mail. Along the way, folks are going to ask you how you're feeling and tell you you're looking awfully well. You'll be interrogated pretty closely about the weather, too. They'll want to know if this is cold enough for you or if you think it's ever going to stop raining. You will have to be ready with some snappy answers.

Simply to gain access to the Post Office is in itself a challenge to one's interpersonal relationships. Let me see if I can describe it to you. There are two sets of doors, you under-stand—an inner set and an outer set. All four doors have panes of glass in them. So, when you're going in, you see the person who is coming out...and you stand holding the door open, and he's standing holding his door open. You start forward—just as he starts for-ward, and you say, "Oh, I'm sorry. You first. Isn't this a gorgeous morning? Thank you, that's very good of you." Finally you manage to get inside.

Inside the Post Office is a babble of voices. The lobby is filled. Conversations are going on. People are discussing just about every-thing under the sun like whether it helps your arthritis to carry a raw potato in your hip pocket and who owns the strange dog

"Simply to gain access to the Post Office is in itself a challenge..."

that was seen walking up Cottage Street and whether the juice plant is still pressing out apple juice. By the time the mail's all sorted, you've got something a lot more vital to take home than these tiresome old headlines about disarmament and nuclear destruction and all that junk. Why, you can collect up enough news at the Post Office to entertain

the neighbours over several rubbers of bridge—really lively stuff, too.

In the lobby of our Post Office hangs a picture of the Queen. It's there, I think, to remind us that we live in a democracy. As a further reminder, we have only to look at our post office boxes.

At the top, are the smaller or regulation size boxes, suitable for the average citizen who receives a weekly newspaper along with the electric light bill and a free coupon for a box of detergent. He (or she) can stand up straight and open his box and take his mail out with something close to dignity.

Now lower down, beneath the regular sized boxes, about three-quarters of the way down are larger boxes, about twice as big. These are for people who are very comfortably off, with magazines coming in, monthly newsletters from their stockbrokers, and lots of those nice long window envelopes. But these people, you see, these more affluent citizens, they have to bend over when they open their post boxes. It's not quite so dignified, especially if they're a little overweight.

Then away down at the very bottom we have the drawers. You have to really squat down to open these. They are for the pulp company, the gypsum company, the big industrialists of our town. We love to see them, down on their hands and knees, pawing about among their dividend cheques. You see, we really do live in a democracy in this country and Ottawa recognizes it.

"...in my home town we don't have postal delivery service... we just have the Post Office."

There is something else pretty wonderful that the people in Ottawa do. They seem to know how to pick out the right people to stand behind that wicket. Take our Postmaster. I'm sure he knows all kinds of incriminating things about every one of us. We've all tried to get away with overweight letters and parcels. Some of us are addicted to wheat germ oil and sunflower seeds which we must purchase by mail order. Oh, there are all sorts of things. Romances have had their start out here in the lobby. The Postmaster just smiles and keeps it all to himself.

In many cases, what could he say? What can you say to an old lady who appears at the wicket twice a day, asking for her mail when there isn't any mail—and hasn't been for weeks—because her family are all dead and gone now.

Then there's the kid who's been hanging around since college closed, waiting to hear from this firm in Alberta who said they *might* have a job for him and, if so, they'd be sending him a cheque to cover his air fare out to Calgary. When the letter comes, he tears open the envelope and takes out the —no— no, it isn't a cheque. The job's been filled. He turns quickly and leaves the post office so no one will see how the colour has drained from his face.

But mostly our Postmaster is a dealer in happiness—in that most priceless of all commodities: hope. Every day, we live in expectation of the letter we've been waiting for, or a notice to call at the wicket for a mysterious parcel. If we're stamp collectors, there is always the chance that the latest commemorative will be the one defective sheet in thousands, worth a small fortune.

Toward the end of the month, there comes that wonderful day of the Government cheques. Everybody is laughing and being handed long brown envelopes and our bank and credit union have to lay in an extra supply of tens and twenties. All the bills get paid, and for two or three days the town is living on porterhouse steaks and sending its wash to the laundry. Then, gradually, it sinks back into a more normal way of living and does its own washing.

In the lobby we have a bulletin board. It keeps us posted on all the latest government publications—things like how to keep hens, and how to build a survival shelter, and what to do till the doctor comes—stuff like that. They tell you about the civil service jobs that are offering, and these are always very interesting. There are lovely jobs for dental technicians, and chief auditors, and postal inspectors. None of us can qualify for these jobs, but we like to read about them. It's always a comfort to know that if we *did* have the qualifications, we could be making thirty or forty thousand a year!

With things like this to divert us, there's no chance for our lives to become narrow or provincial. In fact, at times it can be kind of exciting. You step into the Post Office and suddenly everyone is talking a strange language. You're surrounded by men who haven't shaved in weeks, wearing berets and turtlenecked sweaters, and you know a lumber boat is down at the Government Wharf, loading. All these fierce looking men are members of her crew, sending airmail letters to their mothers, and buying money orders for their wives or sweethearts back in Germany or Sweden or Denmark. This gives us a grasp of the international situation.

The red brick building with the slate roof, and the summertime flower beds out front bright with begonias draws us like a magnet. Few can bear to stay away from it for more than a day, unless they live on the outskirts of the town or up on the hill where you can look down and see the houses dreaming at your feet, with church spires peeking out here and there, and a halo of white wood smoke from the pulp mill drifting across the sky.

Some people live so close to the Post Office that there's no keeping them away from it. It gets to be a habit, like taking tranquilizers. They're dodging in and out two or three times a day, posting get-well cards, operating the little stamp dispenser, and inquiring if the mail truck from Halifax is on time.

Time in our town is a very precious thing. Ottawa understands that and has placed a large electric clock up on the roof so we can all keep a check on it with our watches and make sure it's not running too fast or too slow. It is a beautiful clock. It is illuminated at night so that when the pulp mill workers knock off at midnight and drive up William Street on their way home they'll know it's midnight.

Then except for the clock, the building is all in darkness. It's almost as if the heart of the town had stopped beating.

The flagpole out front is standing bare and silent. But tomorrow morning at eight the maple leaf will be flying once again. Her Majesty's Royal Mail will be waiting for you to come and get it.

POSTSCRIPT

I thought this would be easy. But I was wrong. When they asked me to put on these broadcasts I said, "Sure, I'll do them; why not? I live in a small country town. The whole thing is right there in front of me. It's just a matter of talking about it, and you learned how to talk years ago when you were a kid. This should be child's play." But that's where I made a mistake.

Of course, almost anyone can fill in 15 minutes of talking; I've known people to keep it up for hours, but it takes real staying-power to be the other person they're talking *to*. The patient radio listener is the real user of words—though what he makes of all the words he hears I've never quite fathomed out.

—From a radio talk by Norman Creighton